The Invitation

The Invitation

ORIAH

HarperSanFrancisco
A Division of HarperCollins*Publishers*

For Catherine

"The Invitation" was originally published, in slightly different form, in *Dreams of Desire,* a collection of poetry by Oriah Mountain Dreamer (Toronto: Mountain Dreaming, 1995). Copyright © 1995 by Oriah House. "The Invitation" was inspired by a writing exercise taught by David Whyte at one of his workshops. David based this exercise on his poem "Self-Portrait," printed in the poetry collection *Fire in the Earth,* published by Many Rivers Press.

HarperCollins books may be purchased for educational, business, or sales promotional use. For information please write: Special Markets Department, HarperCollins Publishers, 10 East 53rd Street, New York, NY 10022.

HarperCollins Web Site: http://www.harpercollins.com

HarperCollins®, 📖 ®, and HarperSanFrancisco™ are trademarks of HarperCollins Publishers

FIRST HARPERCOLLINS PAPERBACK EDITION PUBLISHED IN 2006

Library of Congress Cataloging-in-Publication Data is available.
ISBN–13: 978–0–06–111671–1
ISBN–10: 0–06–111671–8

06 07 08 09 10 RRD(H) 10 9 8 7 6 5 4 3 2 1

Contents

The Invitation

It doesn't interest me what you do for a living.
I want to know what you ache for, and if you dare to dream
of meeting your heart's longing.

It doesn't interest me how old you are. I want to
know if you will risk looking like a fool for love, for your
dream, for the adventure of being alive.

It doesn't interest me what planets are squaring your
moon. I want to know if you have touched the center of your
own sorrow, if you have been opened by life's betrayals or have
become shriveled and closed from fear of further pain. I want
to know if you can sit with pain, mine or your own, without
moving to hide it or fade it or fix it.

I want to know if you can be with joy, mine or your
own, if you can dance with wildness and let the ecstasy fill
you to the tips of your fingers and toes without cautioning us
to be careful, to be realistic, to remember the limitations of
being human.

It doesn't interest me if the story you are telling me is true. I want to know if you can disappoint another to be true to yourself; if you can bear the accusation of betrayal and not betray your own soul; if you can be faithless and therefore trustworthy.

I want to know if you can see beauty, even when it's not pretty, every day, and if you can source your own life from its presence.

I want to know if you can live with failure, yours and mine, and still stand on the edge of the lake and shout to the silver of the full moon, "Yes!"

It doesn't interest me to know where you live or how much money you have. I want to know if you can get up, after the night of grief and despair, weary and bruised to the bone, and do what needs to be done to feed the children.

It doesn't interest me who you know or how you came to be here. I want to know if you will stand in the center of the fire with me and not shrink back.

It doesn't interest me where or what or with whom you have studied. I want to know what sustains you, from the inside, when all else falls away.

I want to know if you can be alone with yourself and if you truly like the company you keep in the empty moments.

Accepting the Invitation

ONCE IN A WHILE, we are given moments of real grace.

Sometimes, during my early-morning meditation, a place within me opens and parts of myself let go that I did not even know were holding on. In these moments I feel all the hard places in my heart and body yield to a great softness carried on my breath, and I am filled with compassion for the part of me that is always trying, always organizing, problem solving, anticipating. And my mind stops and simply follows my breath. A great faith washes through me, a knowing that everything that needs to get done will get done. My shoulders drop an inch, the small but familiar ache in my chest eases, and the moment stretches. There is enough: enough time, enough energy, enough of all that is needed. A great tenderness for myself and the world opens inside me, and I know I belong to this time, to these people, to this earth, and to something that is both within and larger than all of it, something that sustains and holds us all. I do not want to be anywhere else. I am filled with commitment to and compassion for myself and the world.

Rising from my cushion, I move unhurriedly toward my day. As I step into the bathroom, I catch a glimpse of the quiet half-smile on my face dissolving into a grimace of disgust as cold water soaks through my clean white socks. All semblance of graceful ease shatters in the shrill cry of the banshee as I survey the aftermath of my teenage sons' showers: pools of water on the tile floor; several wet towels in a heap in the corner, others twisted onto towel racks in configurations that could not possibly dry before the end of the millennium; the shower curtain half in, half out of the tub, bunched and folded to maximize the growth of mildew and mold.

Later, after cleaning up, my younger son, Nathan, speaks to me as I sit in the kitchen with a cup of hot tea. "I know we shouldn't leave the bathroom such a mess, Mom," he says cautiously, trying to sound reasonable, "but I think leaving wet towels on the floor is probably pretty normal behavior for teenage boys. Not that we should do it," he adds hurriedly as I pierce him with a look over the rim of my cup, "but if that's the worst thing we do, you really don't have too much to worry about, do you?"

I can't help but laugh. He is right, of course.

This is the reality we live: aspiring to be at our best, longing for and sometimes finding meaning and connection within ourselves and with that which is larger than ourselves, we are undone by messy bathrooms, traffic jams, and burnt toast. I am not interested in a spirituality that cannot encompass my humanness. I find little comfort or guidance in traditional dogma or unqualified New Age optimism. Because beneath the small daily trials are harder paradoxes, things the mind cannot reconcile but the heart must hold if we are to live fully: profound tiredness and radical hope; shattered beliefs and relentless faith; the seemingly contradictory longings for personal freedom and a deep commitment to others, for solitude and intimacy, for the ability to simply be with the world and the need to change what we know is not right about how we are living.

"The Invitation" is a declaration of intent, a map into the longing of the soul, the desire to live passionately, face-to-face with ourselves and skin-to-skin with the world around us, to settle for nothing less than what is real. This book is a journey into the territory mapped out by "The Invitation." If we are to traverse this territory together, there are some things you should know. Because simply saying "yes" to "The Invitation," feeling the pull of the heart or the quickening of the blood that urges movement forward, is not the same thing as actually making the journey.

I want to live with deep intimacy every day of my life. I am guided, sometimes driven, by an ache to take the necessary risks that will let me live close to what is within and around me. And I am sometimes afraid that it will be too much, that I will not have, or be connected to, whatever it takes to be with it all, to bear the exquisite beauty and bone-wrenching sorrow of being fully alive. Knowing how frightening both the beauty and the pain can be, I offer you here, at the beginning of this journey, three promises that are, simultaneously, three warnings.

First, the places foreshadowed in "The Invitation" are not metaphorical; they are actual. When I say that I want to know if you can get up after the night of grief and despair, weary and bruised to the bone, and do what needs to be done to feed the children, I don't mean I want to know if you have good intentions or if you can afford to pay someone else to care for those who need your attention. I want to know if you really can get up when nothing in you wants to do anything but stay beneath the covers. I want to know if you can do the small, mundane but necessary tasks, if you can give what is needed when you feel you have nothing left to give. When I ask if you can be alone with yourself, I am not asking if the idea of being alone appeals to you but if you can actually be present, with yourself, for longer than a couple of hours, without flipping on the TV or the radio or·picking up the telephone or a magazine, if you can truly find and be at peace with your own company.

The first warning, then, is also the first promise: if this book succeeds in actually taking you into the territory of "The Invitation," you will experience, not just read about, the ache, the sorrow, the joy, the courage, the peace . . .

The personal stories I share here are not important in themselves. We all have a thousand stories, and my life has had no more or fewer than others. But stories, carefully chosen and shaped by both the teller and the listener, can open gateways into our interior landscape, can reveal the meaning in our lives enfolded in the details and unfolded in their telling and conscious contemplation. I promise that I will not pretend to know something I have not experienced. Nor will I try to increase our comfort with each other by feigning confusion where I have knowledge.

This, then, leads to the second warning and promise: the consequences of moments of deep intimacy with yourself, another, or the world are completely unpredictable. When we learn how to truly be present with our joy and our sorrow, with our longing and our desires, layer upon layer of our selves and the world are revealed. We cannot know in advance what this revelation will look like or what action it will inspire or compel us to take. I have watched participants at workshops I have facilitated circle a moment of anticipated intimacy with their own desires, catch the scent of portended change on the wind, and turn and flee the very thing they came seeking—a deeper connection with self and spirit—for fear of what it would call upon them to do in their lives. If we have based parts of our lives on lies, or truths that no longer hold, however well intentioned or unconscious, the changes that deep intimacy evokes can look very dangerous. We cannot tell in advance which aspects of our carefully constructed sense of self, if any, will survive. This is the good news and the bad: if you take the journey, real change is possible and inevitable and, from the present vantage point, completely unpredictable.

The third warning holds yet another promise: no part of the journey is wasted. Once you recognize within yourself a hunger for something beyond just continuing, once you taste even the possibility of touching the meaning enfolded in your life, you can never be completely content with just going through the motions. There is no going back. Learning cannot be undone. The wisdom touched in moments of real intimacy penetrates the soul with knowledge of who and what we are. It transforms us.

I cannot promise that the journey will always be easy. Opening ourselves to living intimately with the world is not a selective process. If we refuse to touch the places of sorrow or confusion within ourselves or others, we cannot cultivate the ability to be completely present in our moments of joy and ecstasy. But if we are open to sorrow as well as joy, we can expand our ability to hold ourselves and the world in our own hearts.

I know we can do this, because I have experienced and have seen in others the ability to go into and embrace each of the places of intimacy invoked by "The Invitation." I can tell you that it is possible to feel pain without moving to hide it or fade it or fix it, to dance with joy and feel the ecstasy completely, to live with failure, to see beauty, to stand in the center of the fire . . . I have lived each of these without regret, and my experiences have given me a great faith in the human spirit. My experiences have birthed within me an infinite tenderness for the courage of the human heart, mine and yours, that will stand up again and again and expand to hold all that matters, even when doing so seems, to the human mind, unbearable or simply impossible.

We can do this. And when we do it together, it is easier. When I was giving birth to my first son, my partner—who was as inexperienced and overwhelmed as I was by the intensity of sixteen hours of labor—tried to reassure me that everything was progressing as it should, that I was fine. Caught between the fear of what was still to come and the pain of the moment, I was not at my best. "How would you know?" I snapped at him, and we both looked to the midwife. When she assured us that everything was fine and reminded us both to breathe, we listened. She knew. She had been there many times before. It was her knowledge, born of experience, that we trusted.

We will give birth here to a deeper intimacy with our lives and our world. I am the midwife who has attended many births and borne children herself. When it is hard, I will remind you of what you already know: that you can do this; that the courage to go deeper is found by letting your desire grow larger than your fear; that strength is found in your longing to live fully, your willingness to settle for nothing less. I will not leave you suspended in the places that may be difficult, but will move you through to the places where breathing comes more easily, periodically offering prayers and meditations you can use to rest and renew your body and heart.

We are not alone as we struggle to open fully to life. When I am able to live with real intimacy, when I pay attention to each moment and do not shrink away from what is true, I experience a presence that is not mine alone, that holds me even as I hold the moment. This presence, this Great Mystery, known by so many different names—God, Spirit, Allah, the Great Mother—lifts me, fills me with a vast silence and a sharp taste of the interconnectedness of all life. I have faith in this Mystery and the many ways in which it sustains us.

Before we begin this journey together, you have a right to know what motivates me, why I seek to live intimately with my own life and the world. The most truthful answer to this is the simplest: because I have to. I am compelled by some deep hunger of the soul, driven by a desire that will not leave me alone, to live life to the fullest. And I know this does not mean working endlessly, accomplishing the most, or consuming the greatest amount and variety of things and experiences. It means tasting each mouthful, feeling each breath, listening to each song, being awake and aware of each moment as it unfolds.

Living fully in the present does not mean disregarding the consequences of our actions for the future. If we in the West, where so much of the world's political and economic power resides, are going to find a way to make the changes that are necessary to ensure that our children's children can live on this planet, we have to learn how to participate fully in our own lives, how to remember and experience the interconnectedness of all spirit and matter. I seek wisdom in a life that combines contemplation and action. Real contemplation—truly being with the joys and sorrows of my own heart and the world—moves me to action guided by awareness and fueled by a passion for life.

There are no deals being offered here. You cannot trade the courage needed to live every moment for immunity from life's sorrows. We may say we know this, but ours is the culture of the deal-making mind. From infancy, we have breathed in the belief that there is always a deal to be made, a bargain to be struck. Eventually, we believe, if we do the right thing, if we are good enough, clever enough, sincere enough, work hard enough, we will be rewarded. There are different verses to this song—if you are sorry for your sins and try hard not to sin again, you will go to heaven; if you do your daily practice, clean up your diet, heal your inner child, ferret out all your emotional issues, focus your intent, come into alignment with the world around you, hone your affirmations, find and listen to the voice of your higher self, you will be rewarded with vibrant health, abundant prosperity, loving relations, and inner peace—in other words, heaven!

We know that what we do and how we think affect the quality of our lives. Many things are clearly up to us. And many others are not. I can see no evidence that the universe works on a simple meritocratic system of cause and effect. Bad things do happen to good people—all the time. Monetary success does come to some who do what they do not love, as well as to some who are unwilling or unable to see the harm they do to the planet or others. Illness and misfortune come to some who follow their soul's desires. Many great artists have been poor. Great teachers have lived in obscurity.

My invitation, my challenge to you here, is to journey into a deeper intimacy with the world and your life without any promise of safety or guarantee of reward beyond the intrinsic value of full participation. To help us along this path, I have offered meditations at the end of each chapter. These meditations are not prescriptions that will fix what is hard or unhappy in our lives and our world, but they have helped me and those I have worked with to expand and live more intimately with ourselves and the world. They can be read slowly into a tape recorder and played back, or followed while a friend reads them aloud to you.

Life lived intimately may not be easier. But it is fuller, richer, and more open to everything: the confusion and the insight, the excitement and the boredom, the shadow and the light. And somehow, expanding my ability to simply be with it all does make what is hard easier to bear, allows me to give and receive more in each moment. More often than not it simply helps me find my sense of humor when I'm taking myself too seriously, to laugh at how easily the wonderful serenity of the meditative moment can be shattered by the mundane sensation of cold water soaking my socks.

I WROTE "THE INVITATION" late one night after returning home from a party. I was unsettled, disappointed with an evening that had been full of the usual social conversation. Restless,

I sat down at my desk in the darkness and listened to the sounds around me gradually diminish as the city settled into sleep. There in the quiet, with a street lamp casting a pale light into the room, I picked up my pen and wrote what I really wanted to say to the people I had met that evening, patterned on a writing exercise I had learned at a David Whyte workshop.

When I was finished, I sat in the half-light and read the words aloud to the sleeping city. I heard my longing to be fully with others. And in the silence that followed, I heard the voice of the world I sometimes think I hear late at night, begging me to remember this longing.

When I imagine myself as an old woman at the end of my life and ask myself how I will evaluate my time here, there is only one question that concerns me: Did I love well? There are a thousand ways to love other people and the world—with our touch, our words, our silences, our work, our presence. I want to love well. This is my hunger. I want to make love to the world by the way I live in it, by the way I am with myself and others every day. So I seek to increase my ability to be with the truth in each moment, to be with what I know, the sweet and the bitter. I want to stay aware of the vastness of what I do not know. This is what brings me to the journey. I do not want to live any other way.

And sometimes, I allow myself to imagine that each moment in which we love well by simply being all of who we are and being fully present allows us to give back something essential to the Sacred Mystery that sustains all life.

MEDITATION FOR BEGINNINGS

Sit or lie down in a comfortable position and bring your attention to your breathing, following the breath as it enters and leaves your body, letting your muscles let go with each exhalation. Do this for a dozen breaths, just following the rising and falling of your body with each breath.

Now, let yourself focus on one thing you want to do that is not currently part of your life. Let it be something specific and concrete and imagine in detail what it would look like, feel like. It may be meditating or exercising daily, learning something new or doing something creative—dancing, painting, writing, singing—or simply being more patient with those you love. Pick something that has meaning for you.

See yourself beginning this activity. Imagine the state of mind, body, and emotions ideally required to begin. How do you want to be feeling mentally, emotionally, and physically when you start? Imagine yourself as you ideally want to be to begin. Stay with this for a few breaths.

Now, be aware of how you are feeling mentally, emotionally, and physically at this moment. Feel the gap, if there is one, between where you want to be as you begin living this aspect of your life and where you are. Imagine two selves: one, feeling as you would ideally like to feel to begin and the other, just as you are, perhaps more tired, less inspired, less calm, or more distracted than you want to be. Let your attention follow your inhalation and your exhalation and take a few moments to feel, without judgment, the gap between where you are and where you want to be—or think you should be—to begin.

Now, imagine yourself beginning what you originally wanted to do, starting from the place you are, right now. See yourself doing it—meditating, exercising, being more patient with someone you love, learning something, doing something creative—just the way you are, perhaps a little tired or distracted or agitated or uninspired. Do not pull away from the way you are feeling. Let yourself relax into how things are and imagine doing what you want to do, perhaps not as perfectly, not as ideally as you first imagined it, but doing it anyway. Let go with each exhalation; let yourself feel exactly how you are feeling. Give yourself permission to begin from here.

The Longing

It doesn't interest me what you do for a living.
I want to know what you ache for,
and if you dare to dream of meeting your heart's longing.

I HAVE FAITH IN LONGING, wherever it finds me. And often it finds me at unpredictable and inconvenient moments. It's like a door that suddenly opens. I am never prepared. There is no preparation for the way it takes me and leaves me, for the fierceness of the ache. It is the voice of the parts of myself I have left behind in the deals I have tried to make with life, trying to trade pieces of my dreams for promises of safety.

Some mornings I take two minutes to sit in my backyard and offer a prayer for the day, even though part of me is anxious to begin the tasks lined up before me: getting my sons up, cooking breakfast, returning phone calls, throwing a couple of loads of laundry into the washer, sending out a mailing . . . .

But just for a moment I sit in the fresh, cool sunlight of the early morning, the breeze moving my hair, my bare feet in the moist grass, and I am surprised by the wave of longing that sweeps over me. It is an unnamable ache. It makes my breath catch, my lips whisper, "I want . . . I want . . ." I can't put a name to it. I have to wait, open and hungry. And it comes and takes me, this longing, and I remember what I thought I could never forget. This longing seduces me with promises embedded in the cells of my body. It whispers to me of rest, of deep connection with myself, of the ache for another, of living faithful to the sacred.

Sitting with Twylah Nitsch, a Seneca elder, at her kitchen table in the pale morning light, sharing cups of hot tea, I ask her, "How long were you married?"

Twylah pauses and pushes back the wisps of white hair that refuse to be confined by bobby pins. She is a tiny woman, less than five feet tall, full of vitality at eighty. The fine lines of life cover the skin of her face and hands. "I *am* married," she replies quietly. "Though my husband died twelve years ago he is still, as he was for the thirty-two years before that, my husband."

The way she says it makes my throat ache. I can see in her eyes and in the way her hand reaches for the carton of cream that it is true. I know that last night, alone in her bed, as she slipped across the borderland into sleep, she felt him curled around her, the soft hair of his chest against her thin back, his strong thighs along the curve of her aging buttocks, his strong hands gently cupping her softly sagging breasts. It is, as it has always been. The separation of years, or even worlds, cannot dull their ache for each other.

Silently, her pale blue eyes watch my face as my fingers trace the sun's patterns on the plastic tablecloth. I long for this depth of intimacy, this level of commitment to another and to each moment of my life.

I want to know how to live this even when our time together is brief. When we meet, I don't want to ask you what you do for a living. I want to know what you ache for when that door of longing swings open and if you have the courage to feel your own desire. Tell me something you have not told yourself for a very long time. Let it come up from your belly, so we can be surprised together. We will sit here, together, for as long as it takes, waiting for it to come. It's hard to wait alone. There have been moments when I was afraid my longing would never find me again. All my journeys have been in search of the desires I have abandoned.

More than a decade has passed since I stood in the living room with my suitcase packed, Nathan drooling good-naturedly, propped on my hip, Brendan playing with some wooden blocks at my feet. I had no plan beyond gathering the diapers and toys and clothes I had packed. I waited for my husband to come home as the shadows lengthened. I was a woman suspended, unable to move even to switch on a light. I hoped he would arrive before it was dark enough to make standing there in the middle of the room without any lights on seem completely crazy.

When he came through the door and glanced at the suitcase, all I could say was, "We're leaving," my voice small and flat.

"Really," he sneered, "and just where were you planning to go?" He was not a cruel man, just a tired one. We were both so tired.

"I don't know. I just know I can't stay here." The words could not express the terror I felt that I was withering inside myself a little more each day.

"Oh God, Oriah, anything for a little drama." He took the boys into the kitchen and started making dinner.

I was alone in the living room, the dying light pulling all the color from the familiar shapes of the furniture. I could not leave my sons, and I had no place to take them. I waited for the familiar numbness to move up my legs and through my body. Eventually, I knew, I would be numb enough to move. And when I was, I picked up the suitcase, walked to the bedroom, and unpacked the clothes, placing the suitcase at the back of the closet.

My husband and I never spoke of that evening. A year later, when I finally did leave, he was shocked. He gave me a blank stare when I reminded him of that night, of how I had greeted him with a packed suitcase—he looked at me as if I was making it up.

And the beginning of the leaving started. In my relationships I became a woman with one hand always reaching for the doorknob, afraid to leave any door closed too long for fear of getting trapped, of finding myself once again standing in the twilight unable to leave with nowhere to go. From the beginning, I told each man what to expect. I could not be found guilty of subterfuge, of misleading anyone. Honesty was my alibi.

I knew I could not stay unless I knew I could leave. Knowing I could leave, I ached to know I could stay, to know how to live a commitment to a mate that did not turn my face away from my own life, inner and outer.

Tell me what you ache for. I don't want to hear one more dysfunctional family history as an explanation for your current human frailties. Let me taste your stories in the salt of the tears I brush from your eyelashes. I long for a slow-motion meander in the getting-familiar places. I want to spiral close, almost touching, to the place where we can feel the heat in the air between us, an unhurried journey as we sift through new scents of each other, letting them linger in our nostrils, breathing them in deeply, allowing our bodies and hearts to taste the impulse to move toward each other before we move.

I want to be courted by the truth. Let the stories that are telling our lives spin out in long multicolored threads. Don't tell me too much, too soon. Don't hide anything. Tell the tales of your heart, offer them like perfect pearls coming up from the depths of the sea to be strung together, each gently clicking against the other, luminous and iridescent as they roll out of the moistness. Ten years from now I want to hear a story of your childhood I have never heard before and know the delight and ongoing awe of seeing each other for the first time, again and again. Give me each picture slowly, so I can sit with it and find you, and the glimpses of me, and the foreshadows of us there in the details. I want to talk in seamless conversation all night long and find ourselves able to hold the silence together for days, our intimacy sharpened by shared solitude.

And if we are to be lovers for the first time or again, after many times, let the lovemaking be filled with shyness and discovery the way it was, or could have been, when we were sixteen: today a kiss that lingers, a touch on the back of my neck that I can feel for hours; tomorrow a light caress across my breasts that makes my breath catch. I want to savor each discovery of touch as the infinite unfolding of the other. I want to slow it all down, to wander around wet, aching for what is to come next, so I will know when I have been fully entered, whether by your body, your story, or just simply the moment that passes between us.

This is the desire of the human soul for the other, heard through the body and heart. It is hard for me to acknowledge this ache. I worry that it might be only marginally worthy—as a means to an end—as a support for my connection to Spirit, my work in the world. But we love Spirit and honor the sacred by the way we touch each other. Even when I am fully present with myself I still hold, deep within, the longing for another and for the world.

The universe is not twice given. The split between Spirit and matter is in our thinking, our way of speaking of it. I touch God when I caress the face of a lover, hold the Beloved when my son's hand is in mine, breathe in Spirit when I catch the scent of the sun on the breeze. The world offers itself to me in a thousand ways, and I ache with an awareness of how infrequently I am able to receive more than a small fraction of what is offered, of how often I reject what is because I feel it is not good enough. Some mornings, sitting for a moment in the backyard, I don't even notice how I have tensed my muscles against the sound of the city's traffic, resisting what I have decided is a marring of the morning quiet. I pull away from it, unable or unwilling to welcome this sound as part of what is alive, as simply the sounds of men and women beginning their day, going into the world to do the work they do to provide for themselves and their children.

Can you see and touch the divine that is in everything? We live in a secular society, with few ceremonies in our daily lives to help us remember and acknowledge the sacred. Robbed of small formalities, we become deeply familiar with one another's humanness. I want a little distance, once in a while, to remind me of what a mystery others are to me, and I to them, to anticipate touching with awe the divine in another.

My grandfather, Baba, stood when a woman came into the room, quietly, confidently, as if it were the most natural thing in the world. The woman could be young or old, pretty or plain, the next-door neighbor or his soft-spoken sister-in-law. It didn't matter. My father, a man caught between two eras, stood some of the time. My brother, as he grew to manhood, never stood. Our generation shunned the social graces as empty gestures devoid of any real meaning, separated from honorable intent, empty movements designed to placate those denied real power in their lives. What honoring of the feminine could there be in rising from a chair if, at the same time, the community condoned a man beating his wife or forbidding her work of her own?

Did Baba feel the old stirrings of the male warrior in his blood, the one who recognized, honored, and cherished the women of his tribe as life-givers, beings who in the very shape of belly and breast held the image of life? Did he mean to salute life and place himself at her service, or was he merely being polite, following rules long since meaningless?

I don't know. Still, when I enter a room and a man stands until I am seated, I feel a part of myself respond, sensing what it might be like to live where what we offer, the place we hold that is larger than ourselves, is seen and valued. I feel how this calls me, not to deny my humanness, but to remember my place in things, to rise and meet the best in myself, and offer it to my people, to be worthy of being Woman, Life-Giver, Warrior, Mother, Sister, Grandmother, Dreamer, Priestess . . .

It's easy to lose sight of the divine in the partner who takes out the garbage, and easier still if he or she doesn't. It's hard to remember to look for and see the beloved in the parking attendant or the check-out clerk we encounter. We need shared gestures, small ceremonies that help us pay attention, that let us see and honor the mystery of the other every day. This is the commitment my soul longs to make to the world.

And I want to stop trying to do this.

It is not the being, not even the doing that exhausts. It is the *trying:* trying to be present, to be awake, to hold the whole world, to be better, more self-aware, more conscious. My hopes for us are real: I want to help create a world where the very idea of toxic waste would raise such a cry of anguish from the people as to make it unthinkable; where we would move, pulled by the heart, to care for the poor, the ill, the dying and despairing without debating whether they are deserving, without fear of contamination, seeing ourselves in each person.

But as honorable as these desires to make a difference may be, I know my motives are mixed. I am afraid that if I am not accomplishing something I will disappear, I will have nothing to offer you when we meet. I want to be able to live for a day, a month, a year—even a life—that wouldn't make a good story. If I have nothing to tell you when we meet and you ask me what has been happening, I want to be fully content with this. I want to be able to occupy my life right to the corners and for this to be enough.

There are places inside me where the soothing balm of rest has never penetrated. I long for a small respite from the reaching, a moment of sweet stillness, quiet darkness, the great silence that can penetrate and loosen the small, hard knots of endless trying. I want to quit running from my own tiredness. I want to be willing and able to move only as fast as I am capable of moving while still remaining connected to the impulse to move from deep within, stopping when I have lost that slender thread of desire and having the courage and faith to wait, in stillness, until I find it again.

This is what I ache for: intimacy with myself, others, and the world, intimacy that touches the sacred in all that is life. This ache, this longing is the thread that guides me back through the labyrinth of compromises I have made, back to my soul's desires. And sometimes I am afraid of my desires—afraid of what they will ask of me, what vision of myself or the world they will offer that may demand a sacrifice of my carefully cultivated way of seeing. If we are never consumed by the transforming fire of our desires, we risk falling in love with the sweet ache of longing, the daydream of "what if . . ." or "some day . . ."

The willingness to live our desires takes courage. So many times our desires have been used against us, used to sell us what someone else wanted us to buy. Moving toward our desire for deep commitment to Spirit, we have been sold blind obedience; opening to our desire to love, we have been sold an abandonment of self; seeking to embrace our desire for beauty, we have been sold everything from cars to clothes, exotic vacations to plastic surgery. We have been sold a lifestyle, when what our soul desired was life.

To taste our longing, to feel the ache, we risk finding our soul's desires. We risk falling short of fulfilling those desires. We risk living our desires fully.

MEDITATION FOR DESIRE

Sit in a comfortable position with a pen and paper nearby. Take three deep breaths in through your nose and exhale out through your mouth, letting your weight drop to the bottom half of your body as you exhale. Let your shoulders drop and bring your attention to your breath, following the inhalation and the exhalation for several moments. If your mind wanders, gently bring it back to the breath. Follow the rising and falling of your belly with each breath.

Now, pick up your pen and paper and begin to write, completing the statements "I want...," "I need...," "I desire..." Do this for five full minutes. Do not judge what you are writing. Let it come freely, this list of what you need, want, and desire. The things on this list may be very concrete or abstract. Try to be specific.

Pause and come back to your breath, again taking three breaths and letting your body relax. Then, looking at what you have written, read the items out loud, one at a time, saying, "It doesn't interest me if I ever have . . . What I really want is . . ." Complete the second statement, without censorship, from deep within. Speak the unspeakable, hear what your heart and soul most long for, without judgment. Surprise yourself. Tell yourself something you do not already know.

The Fear

It doesn't interest me how old you are.
I want to know if you will risk looking like a fool,
for love,
for your dream,
for the adventure of being alive.

TELL ME ABOUT THE TIMES you have played the fool, risking it all to follow the flame of desire. I can ask and listen without judgment, for I too have been the fool.

I fell in love with a man who looked like everything I had ever imagined I wanted: tall with thick, dark hair and soft, brown, intelligent eyes, his open face and muscled body shining with strong, gentle masculinity. And how he made me laugh, at a time when I desperately needed the laughter. My days were filled with sitting at the bedside of a friend who was in a coma on the brink of death, and he filled my nights with tender lovemaking, wrapping his arms around me when I awoke crying out and reaching to pull my friend back from the precipice in my dreams. All my usual cautions about how fast and how far to open my heart and my life to any man evaporated in the heat of desire that reached for him, both hands open, whispering, "Live." I held nothing back. I risked it all. I let myself love and be loved, deeply.

And eight months later I stood with empty arms, an ache like a shard of glass in the center of my chest, my bank account depleted, my pride shattered. I was the fool.

The hard part of feeling the fool is a little different for each of us. How would you finish the sentence "The worst thing anyone could say about me is . . ."? For me, the worst thing anyone could say is that I have been stupid, easily duped, not savvy enough or quick enough to see things clearly. And I was: stupid enough to give him money, to talk of marriage and having more children, to let him move into my home close to my sons. It makes me cringe to admit it. It doesn't matter how it happened or why I didn't see the warning signs. The end, even though it was I who declared it, left me numb. But I was still here, breathing, though embarrassed and exposed. I had shown the depth of my hunger. I was revealed to the world as a woman of deep, untidy passions that could override my usual ability to be an astute judge of character and to make carefully thought-out decisions. I was the fool.

And I would do it all again.

I would not trade one moment of the loving for the assurance of a predictable outcome or protection of my pride. For I learned to discern between heat and the warmth of real intimacy, between power and passion, between intensity and love. I discovered the wholeness of my longing for a mate—the need for a friend, brother, and partner where I had sought only a lover.

I learned that being the fool will not kill me. Why, then, do we fear it so much?

Sitting on the subway one afternoon, I hear someone weeping and wailing softly, "Help me. Won't someone please help me?" It takes me a moment to locate the source of the sound—a tall woman leaning against one of the doors, tears streaming down her face. Everyone else on the train sits staring straight ahead. I approach the woman, lay my hand gently on her arm, and ask if there is anything I can do. Later, when I have gotten her the assistance she needs, fellow passengers crowd around me on the platform asking questions, anxious to know she will be okay. I am surprised. It isn't that they didn't care. They were afraid—afraid of getting involved in something they could not control, something unpredictable that might call attention to or embarrass them. What if the woman had started screaming at me, or lashed out in some way when I had offered help? What if she had needed instant medical attention I could not provide, or someone to take her home and stay with her?

On this particular day I was not afraid. I was willing to do what I could, knowing what my limits were. My desire to respond to the world around me, to simply do what I am able to do with what is right in front of me, was, for a moment, larger than my fear of making a mistake, of being the fool. Often this is not the case.

I don't want to know how old you are. Your age tells me how long you have lasted but not what you have made of the precious time you have been given. Lasting, enduring, is not enough. Tell me of the times you have taken a risk, and how you greet your fear. Do you bully or shame, cajole or argue reasonably, or simply seek numbness in overwork or alcohol or the chaos of emotional drama?

Fear is part of being alive. Sometimes, when we are in a dangerous situation, fear can be life-preserving. It is a natural response to the anticipation of pain and comes from the realization that if we live and love fully, we will feel the losses that are inevitably part of the constant cycle of change. There is a New Age workshop ad that offers a money-back promise to eliminate all fear in your life forever. I asked someone who had attended the workshop if you really could get a refund if you told the facilitators that you had experienced fear after the seminar. She told me that the participants had been warned that they might experience the "illusion of fear" after they took the course, but that it could not be real fear.

I do not think denial of fear will give us freedom from it.

Sitting in the marriage counselor's office with my husband, I clasp my hands together and squeeze hard. I have told him I am leaving. He sits, shoulders rounded as if by a great weight, silently begging me to stay. The counselor asks if I would be willing to postpone my decision to leave for three months. In the silence that follows, each moment stretches to infinity, every sense is sharpened. I can smell the leather of the sofa and my own sweat, hear the three of us breathing and the clock ticking softly on the table. I see my mouth open, lips dry, and hear the single syllable leave my mouth and echo around the room, bouncing off an emptiness inside my chest. This is what fear is like.

"No."

Something inside me explodes in a great silence that eats all sound as the word settles over us like ash after the fire of devastation. What surprises me most in the moments that follow is that the world continues. We are still there, in the room, the walls standing, the sound of the traffic beginning to drift back through the terrible silence, the next breath being taken in the undeniable pull of life continuing. I have less than a thousand dollars. I need a job, an apartment, and good, affordable day care, and I need it all fast. The unknown yawns before me. I know only that I am leaving, that I will not leave my sons, nor will I take them away from their father. I do not know if the aloneness will be bearable, if I will fall flat on my face.

But the longing is larger than the fear, the desire more fierce than the pain. My second husband is a good man; we did not have a bad life. It was simply not *my* life. I had to leave the life I had built and go forward to meet the life for which I longed.

Each time I follow my deepest desires, fear is there wringing her hands, cautioning me with her litanies of what-ifs. I do not try to counter with reasonable arguments about acceptable risks. I no longer try to shame myself into action with admonishments to stop being the wimp, nor do I pretend to be unafraid. I simply move in the direction I have chosen to go, taking care to do the things I know will help me keep the fear at a level that allows me to continue to feel it and yet still keep moving. I put myself to bed early, eat well, sit with friends, take long walks by the lake. I have learned that doing things the hardest way provides no currency to be traded for greater future rewards.

Several years ago I ran a women's retreat where each woman was given an opportunity, in ceremony, to surrender seven things she held as precious in her life, seven ways of seeing herself or being seen by others.

The intent of this ceremony was not to devalue those things we treasure. Many of the things surrendered have value: being a good mother, a loving friend, a diligent worker, a talented artist. But often we have inherited someone else's view of who we are or should be. And sometimes, although we may ourselves hold these values, their dominance in our lives in a particular form does not allow us to live out other aspects of what we love and who we are. The deepest desires of the soul are rarely concerned with the practical details of mortgage payments, pension plans, prior commitments, past honors, or others' opinions.

Minutes before this ceremony, one woman asked me if I could reassure her that she would not leave her marriage if she chose to surrender her attachment to material wealth and to being seen as the good and patient wife. "No," I told her. "There is no such guarantee. If there were, there would be no point to doing the ceremony. I cannot tell you in advance what your choice will be, whether you will look at your husband and your marriage and know that it is a place you truly want to be. Your attachment to money and being the good wife may be all that's keeping you there."

The other women in the room sat uneasily in the silence. "Then why do this at all?" another woman asked. "Why would we risk the unknown changes that this knowledge could bring into our lives?"

I paused and considered it for myself. "For freedom," I said. "I risk it for the freedom, to see what is true, what I really want in the deepest part of myself. I can make whatever choices I want in my life, and I will live with the consequences of those choices. But if I want to live a life close to my deepest desires, I have to risk knowing who I really am and have always been. Knowing this, then I can choose."

You could taste the fear in the room.

The truth is that some days I feel I am ready for freedom and other days I am so tired I don't want the responsibility it brings into my life. I want a rest from choosing, from trying to increase my ability to choose wisely. And then, in a moment of grace, I am given a certainty: if I never did one more meditation, ceremony, workshop, therapy session, course, or cleansing diet, never attended one more meeting or participated in one more community cause, never wrote another line . . . it would be okay. It would truly be okay. For a moment, as I fully feel this revelation, I am free to move toward what I love.

Years ago, a student with chronic fatigue syndrome told me, "I am afraid that if I stop, if I slow down and rest, I'll never amount to anything."

I smiled. "What if I told you that everything you are ever going to amount to, you are right now?"

I knew what she feared. I have done it a thousand times—confused work with accomplishment, frenetic activity with movement, growth, and learning. We are afraid that we will not be enough. All of our deepest desires are our soul's way of calling us back to simply being all of who we are.

Sometimes, when I see others follow their desires, I am surprised to find myself not only unsupportive but angry, threatened. If I have convinced myself that lack of money and the needs of those dependent upon me are the reasons why I cannot risk doing work that is more consistent with my soul's desires, the woman or man who makes such a change and finds ways to meet obligations similar to mine, without financial resources beyond mine, challenges my certainty that I have no choice. Ironically, I find myself, at moments, clinging to a belief in my own powerlessness, a belief that will let me off the hook of responding to my soul's desire. Those who chose a different response threaten the seamlessness of my self-deception.

Desire seeks to push the edge in the places where we have drawn a line in the sand that says, "This is where I will not go, this is what I will not risk." And what is easy for one may be hard for another. Wherever we have drawn the line, the risk of crossing it feels very real. We risk failing to fulfill our desires, being exposed for our deepest yearnings. We risk mistaking one desire for another, only to arrive at fulfillment held in the arms of disappointment. Certain that we ache for time apart, we may walk away from another only to find our yearning unmet in aloneness. Reaching for the other with whom we can share life, we may plunge into a relationship that brings us face-to-face with a loneliness we have never known in solitude. To move toward our desire we have to allow ourselves to be the fool, the one who does not know, who starts again and again at the beginning.

We are not offered guarantees. What we are offered is knowledge of life and ourselves, and if we are awake, glimpses of the wisdom held in the story our life is telling the world.

When I turn my face away from my longing because of my fear of being the fool, I must work to cover the cracks in my resolve to abandon the heat of my desire. But my soul is too aligned with life to give up. Late at night when I am too weary to push away the longing, she comes looking for me, begging me to simply be with her and my fear of her. I can hear her, a small, insistent voice asking me to remember that desire lived brings the ecstasy of falling more deeply in love with my own life every day. And in the moment of this remembering, no risk seems too great.

MEDITATION ON FEAR

Stand where there is some room to move, indoors or out. Stand still for a moment, focusing on your breath, letting the weight of your body drop down to the bottom half of your body. Feel your connection to the ground beneath your feet for several breaths, letting your attention focus on the inhalation and the exhalation.

Now, think of something you deeply desire in your life. It may be something internal or external—a situation or way of being. Close your eyes and imagine the fulfillment of this desire. What would it look like, feel like to have this desire fulfilled? What does your soul want? How would you know if you had it?

Now, open your eyes and pick a spot you can see in front of you—it could be the door to the room you are in or a tree a short distance away. Focus on this place and imagine it as the place where your desire will be fulfilled. Then slowly, aware of how your weight shifts from one foot to the other, how your muscles and bones move, take a step toward this spot, holding an image in your mind of your desire being fulfilled in this place.

Do not move too quickly; remain aware of the feelings that arise within you as you move toward the place where your desire will be fulfilled. If there is fear, feel it, taste it, and continue to move forward, being present with it. Notice the fear or the absence of fear. Neither search for it nor push it away. Simply notice it and keep moving slowly forward, feeling the fear and remembering the desire you are moving toward. If you are stopped by the fear, wait. Continue to feel the fear, but let the desire grow larger than the fear, and then begin to move again. Be aware of how easy or hard it is to wait for your desire to find you again.

Be aware of how tempting it is to try not to feel the fear and move more quickly toward your desire. Be aware of how any attempt to do this creates numbness that robs the desire of its full vibrancy.

When I do this meditation, I am often surprised to find myself less fearful or more fearful than I had anticipated. Repeating it at different times, I discover that my fear is not always the same. Gradually, my ability to feel the fear and move forward increases.

The Sorrow

It doesn't interest me what planets are squaring your moon.
I want to know if you have touched the center of your own
   sorrow,
if you have been opened by life's betrayals
or have become shriveled and closed from fear of further pain.
I want to know if you can sit with pain,
mine or your own,
without moving to hide it
or fade it
or fix it.

EVERY LIFE HAS PAIN AND SORROW in it. It's part of being human.

If, when we meet, there is pain in your life, tell me—I can listen. Tell it simply. If you don't want to tell me how you are, then don't. But don't tell me about your astrological chart or dysfunctional family. Don't shake your head and tell me that a lot of energy is moving or put your hand to your breast with eyes wide and murmur breathlessly about how a lot is coming through you. Tell me something real, in language rooted in the details of blood and bone, heart and mind.

What is the taste, the look, the sound that comes when you touch the center of your sorrow? When I touch my sorrow I hear, from the inside, the sound of hair being ripped from my scalp. I taste blood in my mouth as my lip splits against my teeth. I feel my muscles cramp tight as I curl up, hugging my knees to my chin, trying to be smaller so he will not find me beneath the desk in the dark corner of our tiny apartment. Later, he tries to convince me that all young marriages are like this behind closed doors. And my real sorrow is that for a brief time I abandon myself and try to believe him. I ache for the young woman I was.

I can touch this sorrow when I choose to. And I choose to when a young woman of sixteen tells me, in almost a whisper, of the boyfriend who hits her across the face when she resists having sex without a condom. It lets me be fully with her, without judgment, when she tells me, "It doesn't matter. It doesn't matter what he does to me. I love him." She expects a lecture and is surprised to see tears on my face. I tell her about the young women I weep for—herself, myself—and together we remember that it does matter what he does to her.

If we are strong enough to be weak enough, we are given a wound that never heals. It is the gift that keeps the heart open.

We are afraid of pain—emotional and physical—and we want to believe that there is a way around experiencing our own sorrow, that we can avoid the pain and lose nothing of the fullness and joy of living. It's simply not true.

But it's hard not to move away from pain. When I hear the young woman tell her story of abuse, the bone in the center of my chest aches. When I hear a news broadcast about an underground nuclear test tearing apart and contaminating the earth from the inside, my knees buckle and I sit down suddenly, remembering what it sounded like, years ago, when the side of my face hit the floor. I know that the sound from inside my body as the bones cracked on the tiles and the sound from inside the earth when the blast went off are somehow the same. This knowledge makes it hard to breathe for a moment.

But I do breathe, allowing the sorrows of the world to break my heart over and over, letting the joys make it whole again. Knowing how to do this, finding the courage to take another breath and not close my heart to myself or the world where there is pain, is what I seek to learn—how to love well.

Sometimes, of course, loving well includes acting. We can stop nuclear testing. We can raise young men and women to feel it matters what happens to them, and we can provide safe places for those who are abused or frightened. But sometimes, in the flurry of activity, in doing what needs to be done, we forget that we cannot change the past. The wounds of the past must be tended by more than the frantic activity of "getting on with it."

Recently, two young boys in the United States gunned down classmates at an elementary school. Less than twenty-four hours after the incident, leaders in the community were calling on residents to "begin the healing process" and "move on with life." This is how afraid we are of the pain. Children had killed children.

It was hard even to take it in. The loss was hardly felt, the pain barely acknowledged, and these men and women wanted to move around the grief and sorrow directly to the healing. It won't work. There is no way out but through. A wound not fully felt consumes from the inside. We must run very hard if we want to stay one step ahead of this pain. Exhausted, we try to bury it with drugs, alcohol, over-work, television, physical activity. We are a very creative species—we can use just about anything to anesthetize ourselves. But in doing so, we also remove ourselves from feeling the joy. Life becomes less, and if we are even slightly numb, it is hard for us to find the wisdom we need in our lives and in our world.

It is hard to be with another's pain if we cannot be with our own. Since I was a child I have always felt a deep sense of responsibility to ease others' pain. But I have discovered that often, beneath this genuine and admirable desire, lies an inability to be with my own sorrow. Several years ago, watching a close friend suffer when a brain aneurysm took away her life as she knew it, I wrote in my journal, "I won't ask much. But if you would just let me save your life, perhaps it will not hurt so much to know I cannot save my own."

Even as I wrote them the words shocked me. In what way did I feel my life needed saving?

I cannot save myself, nor those I love, from the sorrow that is part of life. Knowing this, it is tempting to protect myself from pain by simply closing a little to life, especially in the areas where I have been hurt, in the areas that matter most. When my second marriage ended I became meticulous in setting boundaries in my life, many of them valuable, but most inspired by fear of further pain. Oh, I know what you're thinking. But it's not that I have been violated so often. My boundaries skillfully intact, I now win all the border skirmishes I long to lose and remain unentered territory. How to keep the boundaries I need and still be fully with another, this is what I long to learn.

So, I teach what I need to learn. When I lead a workshop I ask participants, at the beginning, to be responsible for asking for what they need and to stay out of one another's circles, to simply be with one another. I warn them: "Sometimes, during a session, a man or a woman will become upset and begin to cry. If your first impulse is to move toward them—don't. Sit with what it is in you that finds it difficult to simply let them feel what they are feeling. What in you wants it to stop? Sit still and see if you can simply be with them in their pain, and with yourself and your reactions, without moving. If, after sitting awhile, you want to offer something—physical contact, a tissue, a drink of water—ask, before you move. Ask the person in distress if there is anything you can do, ask them if they would like you to sit closer—before you move. And if they say no, believe them, even if you think it is their inability to receive comfort that makes them reject your offer. If you try to step into their circle uninvited, I will stop you."

In fourteen years of facilitating groups, I have never had to intervene to stop someone from interfering with someone else's expression of sorrow. Most people are eager for clear boundaries. In fact, one of the reasons people are often uneasy about hearing of another's sorrow is that they feel the very act of listening will make them responsible for alleviating the pain. Deep inside, we know that there is often nothing we can do to ease another's pain, and we don't know how to live with this knowledge.

We live in a culture that wants only the times of fullness, that often denies outright the fading times. We have forgotten that there can be no full moon without the existence at other times of the tiny sliver of light surrounded by darkness. The fullness of summer is held, on the opposite side of the wheel, by the time of the longest night. To be separated from these cycles of the world, from the births and deaths, is to be separated from life itself. But still we work frantically, seeking the knowledge that will put humans outside this natural cycle of blossoming and decay.

Like many others of my culture, I have put great faith in knowledge. Beneath all of my fears for the future I've wanted to believe that knowledge, the accumulation of information and understanding, would save us from destroying the planet or each other, from medical disaster and natural catastrophes, from the emptiness and grief that is often buried at the center of our busy lives. I've looked to scientific exploration, psychological analysis, and spiritual questing. And I have learned a great deal as I've reached for the hoped-for salvation informed by books, educated by schools, guided by gurus, and assisted by surfing the Internet. It's all there at our fingertips: subatomic particle behavior, brain synapse mysteries, astronomical phenomena, mantras and mudras, and movements to cleanse and enlighten. The luminescence of knowledge floods our lives like spotlights in night stadiums, illuminating every corner, every blade of grass and molecule of Astroturf.

It's not that all the learning is wasted. Like many others, I have over the years gained much insight. I understand my neuroses, my demons, my illnesses, my patterns in relationship. And for my diligent efforts I have an arsenal of tested methods for increasing my health, vitality, and awareness. I am a good student. I am a tired woman.

And all the while, deep inside, I know what I have always known: that the knowledge will never be enough.

This is the secret we keep from ourselves. And the moment it is revealed, we become aware of a need for something else: for the wisdom to live with what we do not know, what we cannot control, what is painful—and still choose life.

Wisdom is often born in the shadows, frequently more visible in the darkness than the light. The stadium lights of knowledge that seek to eliminate natural cycles of night and day, death and rebirth, sorrow and joy do not cast shadows—they provide only the steady glare of illumination. We must move into darker places if we are to find the wisdom we so desperately need. We rarely go there willingly, though every life contains its own cycles of grief and celebration. To meet wisdom in these dark places we must be willing and able to hold all of what life gives us, to exclude nothing of ourselves or the world, to tell ourselves the truth. Wisdom will stretch us far beyond where we thought we could or wanted to go. She will show us what we cannot change or control, reveal what is hard to know about ourselves and the world, and tear at the illusions of what we think we know, until we are surrounded by the vastness of the mystery.

And all the while, wisdom asks us to choose life. She does not want us to just continue, to hang on, to survive. She asks us to experience life actively, fully, every day—to show up for all of it.

Often, we are afraid that if we touch our pain we will drown in it. We fear that once we've opened our hearts to wounded parts of ourselves or the world, we will be unable to function normally, because we will be so overwhelmed with grief that all that is good in life will be inaccessible to us. These fears pull us away from the one thing that can unfold the meaning in our sorrow or simply make it bearable to live with it: intimacy—being fully with ourselves, another, and the world.

I learned a lot about how to be with sorrow from my experience years ago with the physical pain of chronic fatigue syndrome. I would have days of lying in bed with a high fever, every muscle in my body feeling as if it were being torn from the bone. My joints ached and my head exploded with migraines accompanied by nausea and vomiting. Movement or distraction only made my condition worse. Painkillers did little to alleviate my discomfort. Some days, it was all I could do to hang on, one breath at a time.

On one of those days I remembered how I had gotten through labor during my sons' births by following my breath in and out of my body. Lying there in bed, I set aside my thinking about the pain—my fear that this would go on forever, my worries about how I would care for my children when they came home, my anxiety about what would happen tomorrow. This mental anguish was simply one more way of trying to avoid feeling the pain. Gently pulling my mind from these thoughts, I focused on being present with the bodily sensations, with my breath. Slowly, I started to relax the places where I had been tensing my muscles in a futile attempt to move away from the pain inside my body. I focused—one breath at a time. The pain continued, but, miraculously, it became bearable.

Lying there alone, simply being, gently stopping my mind from adding suffering to the pain, I suddenly heard the highest, clearest note of song from a bird outside my window. It rippled through the center of my body like an electric current, leaving behind a tingling sensation. The brilliant green of the leaves of the maple tree outside caught my eye, and I breathed in the sweet scent of the breeze that rustled the curtains, billowing them inward like an inhalation aligned with my own breath. All of my senses were sharpened. It was one of the most exquisite moments of pleasure in my life. The pain was still there, but my attempt to be with it had opened my awareness to the breathtaking beauty of life held in the small things right in front of me. For probably the first time in years, I rested. It was the beginning of the slow and steady recovery of my health.

I am not a purist. When I get a headache, I take a painkiller. But I also sit down and rest, instead of barreling on with my day as if the headache had not happened. And when I am in emotional pain—when I am sick with worry about my son as he struggles with school, or aching with loneliness, or hurt when someone I love lies to me—I draw on what I learned about how to be with physical pain. I sit down and focus on my breath. I allow myself to feel the ache in my chest. I unclench the muscles of my arms and legs and imagine relaxing my heart and feeling fully what is there. I struggle not to get busy, not to clean the house or continue my work, not to immediately seek out solutions or solace.

When the pain is large, when I feel I cannot expand enough to hold it, I send out the simple prayer "Help me" and allow myself to relax into being held by something larger than myself. And sometimes I am held by the presence of a friend or family member who has learned how to sit with pain, how to be with another.

And it works. I find the intimacy with myself and the world for which my soul hungers, and in holding another or being held myself, I am able to retrieve the pieces of self I had left behind in my attempts to flee from pain. I find again the hopeful part of myself I divorced when my hopes were dashed. I find the woman who longs for a man, the woman I left behind when the loneliness seemed unbearable. I find again the part of myself that loves the earth as a sacred sister, the part I sometimes try to leave behind when I fear that the pain of watching her devastation at the hands of my people will be too much.

When we learn to be with our pain, we retrieve the parts of ourselves we have attempted to leave behind, and we are able once again to love those parts of ourselves. We find our wholeness and leave behind the impossible ideal of perfection that keeps us from the wisdom we need to live fully and compassionately with our humanness and the world.

MEDITATION FOR SELF-BLESSING

I have written this meditation to be done alone. If you are doing it with a partner, simply take turns giving and receiving. You can change the words in whatever way helps you connect with that which is larger than yourself.

Sit comfortably and take three breaths—inhaling through your nose and exhaling through your mouth. On each exhalation, allow the weight in your body to drop down, and allow any tension or tiredness to flow effortlessly away. Spend a few moments simply following the movement of your breath in and out of your body, watching your belly expand and contract, your chest rise and fall. If thoughts come, gently bring your attention back to the breath.

Now, raise your hands, cupping them in front of your face where you can feel your breath, as you exhale, on your palms. Send your attention down through your body to the earth beneath you. Send out a prayer to Grandmother Earth. "Grandmother Earth, send to me your love for this one, your granddaughter/ grandson (name yourself or the other). Fill my hands with your love and blessing for her/him/myself."

Then, imagine your breath coming up from the earth, through your body, to your heart on each inhalation. On each exhalation, breathe into your hands the love and blessings of Grandmother Earth, transforming your hands into the old and loving hands of a grandmother. With each breath, imagine your hands becoming full with a great, glowing ball of light. You may feel a tingling or a heat in your fingers. Continue until you feel you are holding all your hands will hold, feeling them not as your hands but as the hands of Grandmother Earth.

Now, slowly, when you are ready, move your hands toward the top of your head. Let them gently touch your hair; feel them as the hands of a grandmother who touches the head of the granddaughter or grandson she loves. Feel her love and blessing flow into you. Slowly move the hands down over your face, gently touching your eyes, lips, cheeks, being aware of how beautiful you are to this grandmother. Let her blessing flow into you, and move your hands down over your body. Move to the places you know need this blessing. Let your intuition guide you. Let the love and blessing held in your hands soften the places that are hard within you. Feel your heart relax and expand. Strengthened and held by the blessing of Grandmother Earth, welcome back into your heart those parts of yourself you have tried to leave behind.

Offer thanks.

The Joy

I want to know if you can be with joy,
mine or your own,
if you can dance with wildness
and let the ecstasy fill you to the tips of your
fingers and toes
without cautioning us
to be careful,
to be realistic,
to remember the limitations of being human.

TELL ME ABOUT A MOMENT of joy in your life. Were you able to let it renew your heart, rekindle your ability to live fully? When did you last laugh until your sides ached? Do you dare to lose control and let the joy carry you?

I'm all for these moments of impossible joy—whether they come in the course of an ordinary day or in an extraordinary ecstatic experience. There are some who would have us believe that we have to choose—warning us away from the ecstatic rush of feeling that comes in moments of real magic, admonishing us to focus only on the joy found in ordinary moments. Their warning is understandable. Moments of mystical union can tempt us to spend our lives searching for those peak experiences and leave us unable or unwilling to receive the same joy where it is offered in the simpler experiences, in the taste of a ripe mango eaten slowly or a moment of quiet stillness.

But I am a greedy woman. I want it all. I want the small daily joys. I want to celebrate the birthdays, the graduations, and the days well lived, *and* I want to experience the ecstasy, the vision of wholeness that dissolves my boundaries and lets me taste the God that lives within and around me. I am a blessed woman, for I have had both. And I have learned that the ecstasy of mango juice on my tongue and union with Spirit are not as different as I once thought.

We are having a special meal to celebrate the end of my sons' school term. You can tell it is special because we are eating in the dining room. The table has been set with the Blue Willow china—not really "good" china, but a different pattern and less chipped than what is used daily. I am in that last-minute frenzy of trying to get everything from the kitchen to the table while it is still hot—the turkey, dressing, mashed potatoes, gravy, broccoli, and summer squash. I have shooed the boys and Taras, the man who is sharing more and more of my life, out of the kitchen. Distracted, I survey the table one last time, making sure everything is there before I sit down, and I glance up to see Taras watching me. I am flushed; damp tendrils of hair have escaped hairpins and curl down around my throat. My dress is wrinkled and clinging to my body where it is moist with perspiration from working in the warm kitchen.

Suddenly, Taras is on his feet, grinning and moving toward me from the opposite end of the table. "God, you look beautiful!" he says, surprising me and grabbing me around the waist with a sure, strong arm. "Look at her, boys," he calls to Brendan and Nathan, "doesn't your mother look beautiful?" His unexpected exuberance makes me believe him. He starts singing the wordless melody of the *Blue Danube* waltz and dancing around the table pulling me with him as I halfheartedly protest that the food will get cold. My hair comes completely undone and falls around my shoulders, and I give up. We dance and laugh and the boys join us, twirling around the food-laden table. Finally we stop, exhausted, and collapse, laughing, into our chairs. It doesn't matter that the food has cooled. We sit smiling and quiet for a moment, catching our breath and looking at one another's shining faces.

Joy finds us and lifts us in ordinary moments like this, if we let it. And the ecstasy we feel then, the opening to life, is not really very different from what we find in spiritual questing or mystical practices, although these experiences have their own ways of transforming us.

Going to a retreat led by a friend in a yogic tradition of meditation, I am prepared to surrender to the ancient method, although it is not my usual way of working. For four days I sit opposite another whose only words to me, over and over, are "Tell me who you are." Each time I am asked, I turn inward and focus my intent on directly experiencing the "I am" that is beyond thought and word and action. As I let go of what I think I am, of what I anticipate the experience to be, my body begins to move. My back arches on an inhalation, my shoulders are thrown back, and my face turns up toward the sky with a long sigh that builds to a low moan on the exhalation. My muscles tense and relax in an undulating rhythm. Each time I go into myself the movement is more intense, my breath deeper and faster. This is not what I had expected. I had imagined some kind of serene peace or sense of all-encompassing benevolence, an infinite stillness—not this heat, this surge of power, this explosion of sensation and movement in my body. Gradually I stop worrying about what others might think and open more and more to the direct experience.

And finally—when I let go of the fear—it's like riding a dragon through the night sky. I feel the fire that is myself and more than myself, and I ride the flame. The boundaries between myself and the walls of the room, the floor beneath me, the person across from me, the trees outside dissolve in the heat. All the edges are ash. There is nothing that is not dragon—winged with feathers of turquoise, vermilion, azure. For a moment I am afraid it will tear me open—and it does—and I am the dragon. The joy of no separation fills me, even as the heat continues to sear through me. I am the heat and the searing.

It is easier to talk about dancing around a dining-room table than it is to describe an ecstatic union with the mystery. Metaphor can only approximate what is beyond words. And yet the joy in both the ordinary and the extraordinary is found in the experience of connection, in the place where we receive the belonging that is ours. When I emerged from the direct experience of who I am, I started to laugh. All of my worries about the future and my resentments about past hurts seemed, in that moment, very small when compared to the vastness of which I was a part. In that moment I knew that joy—real joy that does not deny what is hard in our lives—is a choice. Joy finds us when we feel the elation that comes when we know that we belong—to another, to ourselves, to the world, to the Mystery that is larger than ourselves.

When you share your joy with me, you tell me what you belong to. The joy of dancing in the dining room shows me that at the end of the day, after all is done—efficiently or not—I belong to the people I love. Riding the dragon, I taste the joy of belonging to and embodying the very life force of this universe.

Why is it often hard for us to choose joy, even in moments when there are no painful circumstances in our lives? Sometimes I think we simply do not know how. Many of our secular rituals of celebration and relaxation involve moving away from being with what is—numbing out, if only a little, with drugs or alcohol. As one of my students once said, "We don't seem to know very much about how to lighten up without numbing out." Music and dance are obvious exceptions to this, but in our culture we are too often only spectators and not participants in creating and moving to the sound of celebration.

I want to cultivate ways of celebrating joy in my life, and I want to recognize and savor the moments of joy that come. I want to enjoy the full variety of pleasures life holds, even when some of those joys appear to others to be incompatible and contradictory.

I love my home with all of its carefully chosen furnishings: my grandmother's dark mahogany dining-room set with her china cups and crystal arranged behind the cabinet's glass door in the same places she kept them for fifty years; my massive four-poster bed with the white duvet; the vibrant colors of the rooms—dark blues of sky and red-browns of earth. But I have been equally content in my tiny trailer beside a lake in the wilderness. Its small add-on room with rough unpainted particleboard walls and tin-can woodstove are all I feel I will ever need as I carry clear, clean water from the lake, reveling in the simplicity of only two rooms to clean. I have spent five weeks alone in this place, never hearing another human voice, and been content. My secret joy is found late at night when a million stars are reflected in the still surface of the lake. I paddle out, slip down to lie on my back in the bottom of the canoe, and drift on the water in the silence, held by a million points of light above and below, my heart breaking with the joy of being alive on this beautiful planet.

I resist the voices, inner and outer, that tell me I must choose between joys, must pick a set that fits a lifestyle. I want to rejoice in the pleasure of stretching my muscles as I climb onto the roof of the add-on in the heat of the day, sweat pouring down my back, dust covering my jeans, to tar the seams against the rain that will come and then, back in the city a day later, revel in the joys of dressing in black velvet, sheer stockings, and high heels to attend the opera. Sitting in the dark cave of the theater, I dwell in the center of the joy of a single heartrending note sung fearlessly.

Being with joy means being willing to be stretched, to expand to hold it all. With joy, we are stretched to take in the enormity of it all—ourselves, the world, the mystery. And this frightens us. We have been taught that if we have too great a sense of our own largeness, we will lack humility or invite dangerous envy.

One of the most valuable things I have ever been told was "Never apologize for what you do well." And I don't. I take joy in what I do well, feel blessed by my abilities, and look for ways to share the gifts I have been given. And I have discovered pleasure in doing things I will never do well. I play the piano, very badly, without hope of ever playing well. I play because I love to participate in the making of music. I play because it helps me lighten up without numbing out, stops me from taking myself too seriously, and reminds me that there is joy in what I do well *and* in what I do badly. Those I choose to be with intimately are those who can appreciate the joy of both.

And I am careful not to participate, even by remaining silent, in another's efforts to diminish the enormity in our lives. A young woman, jaded by the past and frightened for the future, shrugs and tells me in a derisive singsong voice that she is at that "I-want-to-spend-the-rest-of-my-life-with-you stage" of a new relationship. I wince, stop her, and ask her not to do this—not to tear at that precious place where love is birthed, that magical time when all things seem possible. I ask her to share with me her joy, her excitement, her fear, and her hope that love is possible. She begins to cry. Joy scares her more than pain. Pain is familiar. Joy breeds dangerous hope and the potential for disappointment.

We are so frightened of the pain of disappointment that we often pick at what is new and hopeful, anticipating flaws or failures, robbing ourselves of the joy that lifts our spirits. If we have lived at all, we know there will be trials, that the bliss of new love will be changed and colored by the practical details of life together. We do not need to be reminded that our lover is human, even if, in touching their divinity, we have forgotten it for a moment—life will remind us soon enough.

The enemy of joy is the litany of "not good enough" that picks at what is or might be, finding the imperfections, real or imagined. I am good at this—my perfectionism can tear at what is imperfect but whole, until the whole is in pieces. Part of me runs toward disappointment in an effort to avoid the pain of being sideswiped by an unanticipated letdown. It's just one more way of trying to feel in control. But to feel joy, we have to trust the moment and welcome it in its fullness for what it is. We have to be willing to acknowledge that we are often not in control—and to celebrate the good fortune in this. And we have to feel worthy of having joy in our lives.

Years ago, my mother and I were talking about the high rate of divorce in our culture. "People," she said matter-of-factly, "expect too much these days."

"No," I replied with both a swiftness and a quiet sadness that surprised myself, "they don't expect enough."

We were both right, of course. We often do expect the happy-ever-after romance of the movies and discount the small, imperfect joys of daily living. But we also often expect too little joy in life and settle for less than our souls need to flourish. It's not that I expect to feel happy every day. In fact, I value the elusive kernel of meaning, the often difficult unfolding of the larger story, more than I value fleeting feelings of happiness. But life is very short and precious. We can make any number of good choices to live meaningful, productive, loving lives. Surely the choices that bring us the most joy will be the easiest to sustain, will make it possible for us to contribute all that we are able. And this is not always about making the choices that bring the most immediate gratification. There is a special kind of joy in what is held back and released in full celebration.

Tell me about a joy in your life that came unexpectedly, a moment that you did not even know you were waiting for, that caught you off guard and made you smile. As I left the university one afternoon, excited by the ideas I had been writing and reading about, a thought flashed through me: "This is what I was made for." I stopped in the street, stunned by the joy of it. People passing paused to look at me standing there alone, grinning from ear to ear.

To find those places, inside ourselves and in the world, where we belong, to find that for which we were made and to recognize it—this is joy. I was made to dance around the dining-room table in the arms of a man who loves me, letting the food get cold. I belong to the stars in the night sky and on the mirrored surface of the lake—to the silence of the wilderness in darkness. I was made to ride the dragon. I belong to the ideas I love. I was made to study and learn and teach and write. I belong to all of this and much more—this is my joy. And it is limitless.

MEDITATION ON BELONGING

Sit in a comfortable position with a pen and paper nearby. Bring your attention to your breathing. Follow the rhythm of your breath in and out of your body, being aware of the rising of your belly with the inhalation and the falling of your belly with the exhalation. Allow the weight in your body to drop down to the bottom of your body, feeling how the floor beneath you and the earth beneath the floor support you. Spend a few minutes just following your breath. If thoughts come, gently bring your attention back to your breath.

Then, in the stillness, allow the phrase "I belong to . . ." to come into your mind and complete itself. You may want to write the statement down. There may be an image that accompanies the completion of the statement. Stay with the image and whatever feelings it raises within you. What does this belonging feel like, look like, taste like? If nothing comes, sit with the feelings that this brings.

When you are ready, come back to your breath, following the inhalation and the exhalation for a few moments. Then, allow the phrase "I was made for . . ." to come into your mind and complete itself. You may want to write this statement down. Spend some time being with the images and feelings this statement raises.

Repeat this process, moving from one phrase to another for five or ten minutes. Then sit and read the list. What do you notice? Are there surprises? Are there people or places or activities to which you belong or for which you were made that appear to be contradictory? Is there joy in knowing to what you belong? Is there fear or sadness in not knowing? How much of your life is spent being with the things to which you belong, for which you were made? Are you willing to have more of what brings you joy in your life? Be with yourself and your feelings without judgment.

Betrayal

It doesn't interest me if the story you are telling me is true.
I want to know if you can
disappoint another
to be true to yourself;
if you can bear the accusation of betrayal
and not betray your own soul;
if you can be faithless
and therefore trustworthy.

WE OFTEN LOOK FOR SOMEONE we can trust more than we trust ourselves. Perhaps this is because we know how often we betray ourselves. Years ago, when a close friend lied about me to a mutual teacher, I learned something about how to tell who was trustworthy. This friend was a good and kind woman but often betrayed herself—ignoring her own feelings to accommodate the wishes of others, abandoning her creative work to take care of a series of alcoholic men in her life. Her inability to be true to herself is what made her untrustworthy, unable to tell the truth when it might bring disapproval from an authority figure.

I suddenly realized that the people in my life who are the most trustworthy—those who tell the truth, even when the truth is hard—are not those who always keep their agreements with me. Those who can be faithless—who can bear the responsibility of breaking an agreement with someone when the alternative is to betray themselves—are trustworthy.

As the original version of "The Invitation" was copied and shared by people all over the world, the most frequent change made to it was to substitute the word *faithful* for the word *faithless*. I received phone calls and letters asking, sometimes demanding, that I explain my use of the word *faithless*. People didn't like it. It made them uncomfortable.

It is uncomfortable when someone perceives us as breaking faith with past promises. Yet, if we live fully, it is inevitable that this will sometimes happen, because change is inevitable, and commitments, if they are to remain vital, must be remade and renewed. Often we protect ourselves from the knowledge of broken promises by pretending that nothing has changed. My second husband and I pretended not to notice that it had been years since he had put his hand on the small of my back as I stood working at the kitchen counter so we could stand close, breathing together for just a moment. We did not allow ourselves to wonder why I no longer touched his face softly and smiled into his eyes after we made love. We did not acknowledge that agreements made to share what mattered, to guard each other's solitude, to be kind to each other had been broken a thousand times.

Unconsciously, we make these silent bargains everywhere—in families, spiritual communities, and business organizations. Devotees agree to bury their knowledge of the guru's humanness, pretend not to see how trust has been violated, ideals abandoned. Members of a congregation do not talk about the times in their lives when they cannot find their faith but continue to attend services and profess what they do not feel. For years I worked in a social service agency where the commitment to women's health was betrayed daily by the implicit agreement that a good staff person was one who would sacrifice her own health to do the work.

We betray ourselves when we deny the change that terrifies us, when we maintain the external illusion that all remains the same. If someone names the betrayal, everything begins to unravel. When our denial of what has happened is so deep as to seem complete, the shock of revelation is overwhelming. We feel broadsided, stunned, broken.

When I told my first husband I was leaving, he didn't believe me. He could hardly be blamed. Neither one of us had acknowledged that his violence was a betrayal of our marriage. We wanted to believe that things could stay the same, and we had made a silent agreement to pretend they were. He looked at me and in all sincerity said, "You can't leave. We're married. You're my wife."

And I said, "Watch me."

Leaving, breaking my promise, betraying his trust that no matter what happened I would not leave—this cost me. Something inside of me was damaged, as I broke faith with our belief in unconditional commitment. Rationally, I can argue as well as anyone that his violence nullified our agreement, and I would never advocate that a man or a woman stay where their body or soul is at risk. I have never been sorry I left. But none of this changes the fact that when we break an agreement we are deeply affected, wounding ourselves even as we wound another.

When we acknowledge betrayal and take responsibility for our decisions to break agreements, for our knowledge that someone has broken an agreement with us, we ache with the anticipated loss of innocence. To trust again, we must be willing to face the shadow of innocence—the deliberate naivete that clings to denial and rejects the truth as too hard.

It has taken many years for me to live consciously with the truth about my marriage: that I did betray my promise to my husband, justified in the minds of many or not; that the abuse in that marriage made me wary of trusting again, unsure of my own abilities to judge when it's okay to trust or when I am really at risk and should leave. I must be willing to live with all of this self-knowledge if I want to be able to love fully again. Pretending that we are not betrayed or that we are not betraying another may seem to make the betrayal easier to bear at the time, but learning to live with the truth is what opens the door to the wisdom required to trust and be worthy of trust again.

Years ago, counseling a woman whose husband had begun a relationship with another woman during their marriage and consequently left, I heard, beneath her understandable rage, the story of a man unable to face his own need to change past agreements. When he finally left, he told her that for two years before the breakup, each night returning home from work, he had driven around the block for ten to fifteen minutes before he had been able to pull into their driveway. In this same period, much to her surprise, he had insisted on cooking all the dinners when he arrived home. It was only as he left that he told her he had done this because he literally had been unable to swallow food that she prepared.

If we cannot live with our need to renew agreements we have made, we break the only promise we really owe each other—to be truthful. This means finding both the courage to be truthful with ourselves and a way to live with how our actions affect others, even when there is no ill intent and no one to blame.

Sitting in my living room, I reach out and hold Roger's hand as he struggles to tell me what he feels he must do. His wife, Catherine, is a close friend of mine. Five years ago, when Catherine was forty, an aneurysm in her brain burst, leaving her mentally and physically disabled. She now moves slowly with the aid of a cane. She must have someone in attendance twenty-four hours a day. She cannot drive or shop or cook or clean for herself. She still forgets where she is and what has happened to her. In many ways she is no longer, nor will she ever again be, wife to Roger, although she calls him her beloved and has clearly not forgotten their love.

Roger has been there with Catherine every step of the way and has only recently arranged for her to live in a group home, giving him some small freedom from making endless arrangements for a succession of daily caregivers. Watching them together simultaneously lifts and breaks my heart. With infinite patience and tenderness, Roger has dealt with the tragedy that has struck both of their lives, taking care of Catherine, seeing to all the medical and logistical details while making a living—all of this while grieving for the lover and partner he knew and letting go of their dreams for a home and children.

And all of this has taken its toll. Lately, each time I see him, Roger looks more tired and drawn, pushed to some kind of breaking point. I wonder how long he can continue with things as they are. On one level it does not surprise me that he sits across from me now, barely able to speak, and says, "I need to ask Catherine for a divorce."

I support him, and I ache for Catherine. This marriage, as much as it is not the partnership it was, is the last vestige of the life that was taken from her. Their love for each other has never died, and Roger has never neglected caring for Catherine, even when he met and fell in love with another woman—a wonderful woman who is torn between her love for Roger, which supports him in his commitment to Catherine, and her own needs and desires for a home and family. She has not asked him to divorce Catherine. She does not ask him to stop loving Catherine or making sure she is taken care of, and yet she wants, as Roger does, to create a marriage of deep commitment together.

There is no place for this story in our culture, no easy and acceptable way to acknowledge the man who loves and cares for his disabled wife while loving and living with another woman with whom he wants the full and committed relationship of husband and wife. There is no point in saying that there should be a place for this story—that in another time or culture there might have been. The individuals involved, and their friends and families, are part of this culture, here and now. Most important, there is no place for this story within Roger, and trying to live it is tearing him apart; it may well result in a breakdown from which he cannot recover.

We sit and cry together. There is no one to blame. Roger speaks in a voice choked with emotion. "I just keep thinking . . ."

he pauses to swallow and struggles to continue, ". . . of what people say . . ." his voice rises in a wail of grief, ". . . of how people say that men don't stay."

There is no easy solution. To survive, to live, Roger must break faith with the promise he made to Catherine years ago, and, if he is to love and trust again, he must find a way to hold himself in his own heart as he does so. And this means finding a place in his heart for all the men and women who don't stay, who leave the job, the community, the convent, the teacher, the organization, the spouse to save their lives—all those who are seen by some as faithless.

We have all been the betrayer and the betrayed. If we cannot acknowledge this, we will find ourselves harsh and unforgiving, unable to grieve for the times we have betrayed ourselves. Only one man has spoken in judgment of Roger's choice. A relative of Catherine's, he told Roger angrily, "You play the hand you're dealt." I wonder what agreements this man has not allowed himself to break, where he has paid too high a price, has betrayed his own soul in an attempt to keep things the same, to avoid the discomfort of being seen as faithless.

When an agreement that is important to us is broken, we feel hurt and angry. And if an agreement is broken but we or others pretend that it has not been violated, we learn to distrust ourselves or those others when the truth is revealed. The real damage of betrayal is in the lies we tell one another and ourselves, the lies that cause us to lose faith in our ability to recognize and act on the truth.

Part of being trustworthy is being able to recognize when our perceptions and judgments are untrustworthy and to cultivate a community that can support and guide us in those times. Years ago, when I was deeply and blindly in love, the man I was with wanted me to give him my credit card. I was charmed, mesmerized by his arguments, convinced by his need. But on the way out of the house to go to the bank, I paused for one second and called my friend Ingrid. Telling her what I was about to do, I asked, "What do you think? Does this sound okay to you?"

Ingrid paused for a moment and then spoke slowly. "Well, I don't know. But I can tell you that you don't sound like yourself, so don't do anything right away. Wait. See how you feel tomorrow. You can always go then. You just don't sound like yourself."

Wise woman, my friend Ingrid. Had she said, "Are you crazy? This man is probably trying to dupe you. Tell him to forget it!" I probably would have become defensive and done it anyway. So she stuck to what she did know: I did not sound like myself, so it was an unwise moment to make this kind of decision. I knew enough about myself to know that I was most untrustworthy in the kind of relationship I had with this man. So, following her advice, I waited. By the next day, feeling more myself, I wisely decided not to give him my credit card.

Being trustworthy, not betraying ourselves, is, in part, about recognizing moments or situations when we are likely to be untrustworthy and seeking the counsel of people who love us and are willing and able to be honest with us. This may mean that we will sometimes hear things we do not want to hear. It almost always means slowing things down a little and considering that we may be wrong, that we may not be trustworthy in that moment.

Refusing to betray ourselves is not a license to break agreements on a whim, to disregard the very real repercussions of our actions on others. The hard part, the place where we hope wisdom will find us, is in deciding where and when we must break a promise to be true to ourselves. We must weigh the cost to our soul if we keep our agreement—the cost to that which is essential to who we are—against the cost to others if the agreement is broken. This is especially true when those with whom we have made agreements are dependent upon us. I could not say that a parent should never leave his or her child, but to break the agreement to be responsible for those we bring into the world while they are young could be justified only if it were necessary in a spiritual or physical life-or-death situation. As in Roger's situation, these are the impossible choices we may be required to make. I cannot judge someone else's struggle with his or her unique choices.

Sometimes, we may decide to make a sacrifice for another. Ask any parent about the small daily sacrifices. Decisions that cost us something important that are made for love can be the soul's choice.

My best friend, Linda, has been there for me, and I for her, for nineteen years. She was present at the birth of my sons; I stayed close during the death of her mother. She had promised not to leave this city, where I am bound by my sons' need for both mother and father. But when she was diagnosed with cancer I told her to go, to leave for the mountains and the ocean, the places that called to her, where her body and soul could be healed. I asked her to break her promise to stay. I asked her to run toward life, even though it took her away from me.

These are the choices we make, consciously or unconsciously, and yet ultimately, if we can be still enough with what is, we can find the place the Native Americans call *Chui-ta-ka-ma*, the place of choiceless awareness, the place where it is clear which choice is a choice for life, where we can make no other. Sometimes, to choose life, we must break agreements; sometimes we must keep them although they are hard to keep.

Tell me, can you do this? Can you make the choice that's for life even when that choice is hard, when doing so means others will see you as faithless? Can you make the choice without putting yourself or the other person—no matter who is the betrayed, who is the betrayer in this moment—out of your heart? This is what I want to know. This is what I want us to learn together, to teach each other in the way we hold each other when the choices are hard.

MEDITATION FOR DISCERNMENT

Sit or lie down in a comfortable position and bring your attention to your breath, following each inhalation and exhalation as it moves in and out of your body. With each exhalation, let go. Let any places in your body where you are holding on simply dissolve with the exhalation. If thoughts come, let them slide away like pearls on silk, and bring your attention back to your breath. Do this for a few minutes, stilling your mind, relaxing your body.

Now image yourself, in your mind's eye, alone in the center of a circle—it may be a circle of light, or fire. It may be a circle marked by a fence of wood or stone, or a moat of water, or a grove of trees. In some form, see yourself standing alone, surrounded by that which marks the boundary of your personal circle. Somewhere in that circle, there is an opening, a gateway of some sort through which others can enter and leave your circle, and at this opening there is a guardian. See the figure that stands at the gateway to your circle—it may be a person or an animal. Let your imagination show you your guardian.

Now, imagine that there are people you know approaching the opening in your circle. As they approach, one at a time, the guardian at the gate will let you know in some way if they should come into your circle. The guardian may indicate this by a gesture, or a word, or a body sensation that you receive. Wait for it. The guardian may indicate that some can come and go at will while others can enter only at certain times and for limited stays. Spend some time learning what the guardian has to show you about the people or situations in your life. Situations may be exemplified by symbolic figures—a colleague who approaches, not as an individual but as the symbol for a specific work situation. Just watch what happens with as little judgment as possible, beginning with uncontroversial individuals or situations (although there may be some surprises here) and progressing to those that have more ambiguity.

Let your imagination flow. Later you can analyze and examine what you receive. When you feel you have all you are able to take in, thank the guardian and bring yourself back to an awareness of your breath and your body, wiggling your fingers and toes and being fully present.

Beauty

I want to know if you can see beauty,
even when it's not pretty,
every day,
and if you can source your own life
from its presence.

MITCH BRINGS SARA FLOWERS, a magnificent bouquet of color: purple and scarlet gladiolas, exotic birds of paradise, and orange tiger lilies, all surrounded by fragrant boughs of eucalyptus. He brings flowers every Friday evening when he comes to share the Shabbat meal. Sara greets him at the door and receives the flowers into outstretched arms with exclamations of delight. A tiny, dark-haired woman, she buries her face in the flowers, reveling in their scent and shapes and colors, examining each blossom. She thanks Mitch again and again, telling him how wonderful he is, how sweet, how thoughtful, how cared for and special she feels.

Mitch grins uncontrollably as Sara kisses his cheek. "You've changed," she says with real pleasure, stroking the front of his freshly laundered shirt. His ears turn red beneath the ends of his curling, still-damp hair.

"Of course," he says quietly. "I wanted to look . . ." he hesitates, embarrassed, ". . . nice for you."

She reaches up on tiptoe to kiss him full on the mouth. "You do. You look beautiful."

Mitch walks to the table where I am sitting. A man of thirty-nine, he suddenly looks like a boy of sixteen. He is glowing, and I could swear that he has actually grown taller during this exchange. The weariness held in his shoulders from working all day at a job he dislikes is gone. His eyes are bright with confidence, and I know, as I watch his eyes follow Sara's movements as she prepares the evening meal, that in this moment there is nothing he would not do if it would please this woman.

Sara recognizes the beauty this man brings her, and she is willing and able to receive it, to let it renew and rejuvenate her. And as she does, the beauty is multiplied. Mitch, fully received, feels something of his own beauty and has more to give.

It sounds simple enough, and it is. But what is simple is not always easy. Sometimes, in our familiarity with the beauty of the landscape of our daily lives, we fail to see it, we forget to really take it in, we neglect to express our appreciation and really let it feed us.

The Navaho have a prayer:

May I walk with Beauty before me.
May I walk with Beauty behind me.

May I walk with Beauty above me.
May I walk with Beauty below me.
May I walk with Beauty all around me.
As I walk the Beauty way.

What is this Beauty that the Navaho seek? It is what pulls us toward life. It is what calls to us when we despair, seduces us into opening again and again to the possibility of love and laughter. It is the physical manifestation of the Mystery—God, Spirit, the Divine—that surrounds and beckons to us every day of our lives. It is life that chooses life. The Navaho prayer expresses our souls' desire to recognize and receive beauty, knowing that as we do so we become co-creators of this beauty, of that which urges, "Live."

Many spiritual paths—both traditional and New Age—posit a hierarchy of beauty. If they give any recognition to the sacred as it is manifest physically, such acknowledgment is confined to the nonhuman natural world and relegated to a status below that of the "purer" beauty of the human spirit or mind. Often, being in physical form is seen as a trial, a burden to be endured, a time to learn vital lessons for the time when we can escape the limitations of our bodies and graduate to the "higher" nonphysical afterlife.

I don't know what happens when we die. But I do know what happens when we live with this separation of spirit and matter. Beauty becomes merely physical packaging, and those with power define what is pleasing based on profitability and subjective preferences. It is easy to become cynical about how the marketplace has used our desire for beauty to sell us a narrow version of what cannot be bought or sold. We know the costs of this: eating disorders, self-hatred, endless striving for physical perfection. It's tempting to protect ourselves from this manipulation by devaluing the physical as meaningless or less important than the emotional, mental, and spiritual. But this perpetuates the split that is so familiar. This separation of spirit and matter leaves us with a spirituality that lacks the vitality and fire of the physical, and expressions of our creativity and sexuality are cut off from the depths of our hearts and meaning of our souls.

Physicality is a gift. It lets us literally touch one another. I am not interested in theories or practices aimed at getting out of here. I do not want to focus on preparing to go to heaven or evolving into formlessness. I want to learn how to be here fully, in this body, in this world. And I want to live in a world infused with the power of the erotic—physical sensation, inseparable from heart and soul, that calls us to live. When we live erotically, the meaning enfolded in our very cells is unfolded as we touch and are touched. This is beauty.

Seeing beauty is not about narrowing our vision, designating only some of its manifestations as worthy. It means expanding our definition of beauty, suspending our judgments, and appreciating both the quiet joy of riding a bicycle along the lake and the raunchy glee of driving a cherry-red sports car that hugs the open highway. It means accepting the truth of being a middle-aged woman as it is reflected in both the lines and sagging muscles of my face and belly and the shine of my eyes.

Seeing beauty is about broadening our ability to recognize the interconnectedness of all manifestations of life and delighting in how the smells and sounds and tastes and sights that surround us conspire to draw us toward living fully. I want to touch the power of life-giving moisture and recognize the smell of the sea where it caresses the shore in the scent of my sweat, in the salt of my tears, in the slippery wetness that pours from between my soft thighs when I am well loved. I want to focus on my fingertips, on the shape and weight of my hand, on blood and bone and a thousand nerve endings, as I raise an apple to my mouth, let the tip of my tongue slide on the round, smooth firmness of the cool surface, and feel the spray of juice as my teeth pierce the skin and enter the crisp flesh inside. I want to taste the weeks of rain and sun, the ripening on the tree, the labor of the farmer and the fruit picker, the journey of the men and women who bring fruit from grove to table. I want to receive the beauty that reminds me that there is no separation—that each act I live while I am fully awake cannot help but be both prayer and lovemaking.

We find and are fed by beauty in the places where the truth—pretty or hard—is revealed in physical form. Sometimes we need help and support to get to the truth. Several years ago, while facilitating a painting workshop, I urged a woman to paint what she felt about her mother's recent death. I knew she didn't want to and that she was angry at my nudging her toward it. I also knew that she would not be able to paint anything else, that she could not go around what was true. The painting that emerged had excruciating beauty in its stark truth. The haunting, terrified figure in the painting clung with bony fingers to a small purse, clutching to something that could no longer help her. None of us could say we "liked" the painting, but we could not tear our eyes away from the beauty it held. It simply was the truth.

Our soul's longing calls truth to us. And even when this truth is hard, when the beauty it reveals is not pretty, our deep hunger for the truth is satiated and some tension deep within us is released. Anyone who has uncovered the lies of someone they love knows how the pain of betrayal comes mixed with the relief of finally being able to acknowledge what they have known but pulled away from for years.

Finding and acknowledging the truth is not always easy. Sometimes—often—we don't know what is true. Of all the phrases frequently used in the New Age movement, I think the one I dislike the most is "This is my truth." I have heard this phrase used to justify blatant self-importance, delusion, and disregard for others so often that I wince when I hear it. I understand what people are trying to say when they use it. It is a reminder that in our ordinary consciousness we have no access to absolute truth, cannot claim that our way of seeing has a monopoly on knowledge or wisdom. It is an attempt to find our own inner authority, to resist giving over the authority in our lives to something external—church or state, family or business—all those voices that profess to know what is best for us.

But in a legitimate effort to claim authority in our own lives, we forget that there is reality beyond our limited perception—if not objective, at the very least, intersubjective. If I get up tomorrow and see two suns shining in the sky, the first thing I will do is ask someone else what they see. If they do not see two suns I will probably go to the eye doctor, assuming something is wrong with my eyes. I will not insist that "my truth" involves there actually being two suns in the sky.

We can be and sometimes are wrong. Knowing this, we can create community where we can check to see if our perceptions have any intersubjective truth. Of course, ultimately, we must decide which perceptions we will grant validity. But to insist that "my truth" and "your truth" have no meeting place, that I do not need to consider other perspectives—to be unable to imagine that I may be wrong about what I think or see or feel at any given time—is to invite narcissistic mayhem.

Nowhere is this more prevalent and dangerous than in the psychological and spiritual communities that focus on personal growth. I am often discouraged to see intelligent men and women suddenly put their thinking minds on hold and accept unfounded conclusions without evidence or explanation. There are truths that cannot be proven by empirical sensory data, but we risk wandering far from any truth if we do not at least ask ourselves honest questions: Did anyone else see the flash in the sky that you took to be a UFO? Why do you think that the voice that came during meditation was the wise guidance of a spirit guide external to yourself? Are there any other possible explanations?

It is easy to fool ourselves into believing the most exciting story. I want to ask the people who profess to know that their beliefs are true *how* they know this. I also want to ask the people who maintain that others' beliefs are impossible how they can be so sure. I have had dreams that have included information—names, dates, places, and events—I can historically verify, information I could not have known from my waking life. Are these past-life memories? They could be, or they could be a result of somehow tapping into a collective unconscious, or being given something from Spirit. I don't know. What I do know is that these dreams feel important, so I explore why these stories—of all possible stories—come to me, what they may have to show me about living fully. I want to unfold their meaning, uncover their particular beauty, the truth they hold that helps me live right now.

I have faith in the truth, in its ability to find us. One of the warm-up exercises I often have workshop participants do is to write a lie, as if it were true, about why they are in the group. People go to great lengths to concoct elaborate lies, and we have great fun sharing the stories. But more often than not, no matter how far away from the facts of their life each person has gone in their story, some truth emerges about why they are there: the woman who writes that she is from Jupiter reveals her feeling of always being the outsider, the alien, in groups; the man who tells us he is an undercover cop often feels he is a fraud or a phony, secretly using others for covert purposes. If the truth often seems elusive when we seek it directly, perhaps it is some consolation that it also relentlessly reveals itself to us in our lives, our dreams, and the stories we tell one another.

It is gratitude that expands my ability to receive beauty in my life. Lately, as I step into the shower each morning, I say a prayer of gratitude for the abundance of hot water that pours over my body, and I ask the water spirits to cleanse my heart as my body is washed. I am awed at the fortune in my life when I think of how, in most times and places, only a privileged few—the wealthiest, the most powerful—have been able to afford this pleasure that most ordinary people in developed countries take for granted. The gratitude I feel opens me to this small moment of beauty in my life.

There are thousands of moments like this in our lives every day. And it is often our awareness of the truth in others' lives that enables us to appreciate beauty when it is offered. Watching a disabled friend labor to cross a room with small, slow steps reminds me to be aware of and grateful for the strength in my legs, the effortless way I move. The story on the news of the woman whose son has been killed in a drive-by shooting makes me grateful for my sons, for their laughter at the dinner table. The truth of her bottomless sorrow calls me to greater patience with messy rooms and neglected homework. And, if I am fully with the truth, I am able to receive and be fed by the beauty in both my friend's pain and perseverance and the grieving mother's courage.

This is how death—the inevitable cycle of change in our lives—becomes our ally. Our anticipated loss of what we take for granted reminds us of what is precious, of what matters and what does not, of the meaning and pleasure of being in physical form.

Tell me, can you see beauty? Can you let it renew your commitment to life, every day? I don't want to wait for death to be near to receive the beauty in my life. I want to be awed every day by the truth—pretty or painful—and let it open me to the beauty that surrounds me and draws me deeper and deeper into my own life.

MEDITATION ON GRATITUDE

Sit or lie in a comfortable position. Bring your attention to your
breath, following the inhalation and the exhalation as it moves in
and out of your body. Be aware of your belly rising and falling.
Let go with each exhalation. Send your breath into the places in
your body where there is tiredness or tension, and let it melt
away with the exhalation. Let thoughts drift away, gently bringing your attention to your breath.

Now, be aware of the physical abilities you have.
Imagine your breath flowing into the parts of your body that
come to mind, one at a time, sending appreciation with your
breath into these parts of your body. Breathe into your feet and
legs gratitude for their shape, their sensation, their abilities that
you so often take for granted. Breathe into your hands and be
aware of all they do each day. Breathe into the places in your
body that give you pleasure, the places that let you touch or be
touched by another, that offer you the taste or smell or sight or
sound of that which brings you pleasure. Breathe your gratitude
into these places, one at a time. Breathe into the internal organs
that keep you alive—the heart that beats steadily, the lungs that
replenish your body, breathing out toxins, breathing in life-
giving oxygen. Remember your digestive organs that nourish and
strengthen your body, without any thought on your part, breathing your gratitude into them.

Breathe into your face, becoming aware of the bones,
the muscles, the skin, feeling the shape of the face by which you
are known. Let yourself appreciate the beauty that is there; take

in the stories of life that are told in the lines and shape and texture and color of your face.

Now, let your mind remember the parts of your body of which you are critical, the parts that are not the way you would like them to be and the parts that are ill or disabled. Breathe them into your heart with appreciation for how they are also a part of who you are.

Move your attention now to your immediate surroundings. Keeping one part of your attention on your breath, breathe in whatever beauty is around you, and breathe out your gratitude for this beauty. Breathe in the color, the temperature, the shapes around you—those that are pleasing and those that are harder to appreciate. Breathe out gratitude for the variety, for the time and the space to do this meditation.

Move your attention to the people in your life—past and present. Breathe in the essence of what they have offered to you—that which has been easy and that which has been difficult. Breathe out your gratitude for them.

When you are ready, bring your attention back to the breath as it moves in and out of your body, moving your fingers and toes, offering a prayer of gratitude for life itself and being fully present.

Failure

I want to know if you can live with failure,
yours and mine,
and still stand on the edge of the lake
and shout to the silver of the full moon,
"Yes!"

ON MY FORTIETH BIRTHDAY I made a vow. I promised my-self that in the second half of my life I would make only *real* mis-takes. Real mistakes are genuine errors in judgment, choices that can be seen, with the knowledge of hindsight, not to have been the best. It's not that I hadn't made lots of real mistakes in my first forty years. But I was frustrated less with those honest failures born of inexperi-ence or lack of information, than with the mistakes I'd made because I'd second-guessed initial judgments.

Several years ago I was asked to co-facilitate an international conference with two women I did not know. I had heard of their work and read a book one of them had authored. During the conference preparations I had an uneasy feeling, which I expressed to both the organizer and the co-leaders. We all worked in very different ways, and we seemed to lack a clear common vision of the conference's purpose and structure. They seemed unconcerned, and I wondered if I should withdraw altogether, but I was plagued by doubts. These women were experienced conference facilitators. Surely they would sense if something was not in alignment in our preparations. Perhaps I was just feeling nervous about co-facilitating; I usually worked alone. Maybe I was just reluctant to trust others, or was trying to be in control. Maybe I needed to learn something about working in a team, with a structure that was more fluid and less predictable than I was used to. It was too late to back out.

As three hundred people assembled, it quickly became clear just how much we facilitators lacked a common vision. Different participants had arrived with incompatible expectations. With no clear structure, method, or purpose, the other two facilitators and myself were unable to work together to stop the most vocal participants from simply bullying everyone else into following their agenda.

My friends and I now refer to this weekend as "The Conference from Hell." What is difficult to acknowledge is that I saw this mistake coming and second-guessed myself, went against my own intuitive judgment. It wasn't that I had not seen the truth. I had. But I'd failed to find the courage to act on it. Of course, my intuition can be wrong. But making a wrong decision, acting on an intuition that is inaccurate, is a *real* mistake, one I can live with more easily than the mistake of failing to act on what, to the best of my ability, I know.

Some deny failure, insisting there are no mistakes. But the inability to admit failure robs us of the chance to learn. To learn, we must be willing to make mistakes, and we must be willing to own our mistakes and learn from them. This is hard for those of us who struggle with our perfectionism. I like to learn things that I know I can do well—preferably, perfectly—quickly. This unwillingness to make mistakes has stopped me in the past from learning new languages. There is simply no way to learn a language as an adult without making thousands of mistakes that are readily apparent—and sometimes very entertaining—to those who know the language. That's how we learn: by trying, failing, receiving correction, and trying again. We all have different areas where it is hard for us to let our mistakes be seen. For me it is languages, because I am attached to my sense of self as intellectually competent. It's just simple self-importance: I hate sounding stupid. However, never having identified myself as someone with athletic ability, I am fine with learning a physical skill, though I will necessarily make hundreds of mistakes and appear awkward as part of the learning process.

When a spiritual teacher nods sagely and says, "There are no mistakes," alluding to a grand design and a higher power that is somehow in charge of all that is happening, it's tempting to agree. There are times when a mistake results in a chain of events that lead to wonderful outcomes well beyond those reasonably expected according to random chance. There are some scientists who assert that the very evolutionary process of creation from the coincidence of survival-enhancing genetic mutations (mistakes) defies the laws of averages and could not have happened by random chance.

I have lived a life full of this sense of unfolding magic and have often felt guided by something larger than myself, sometimes through and often despite my mistakes. When I made the mistake of agreeing to go away for one last weekend with a man I did not intend to see again, I was introduced to a friend of his, a wonderful woman who runs a retreat center that became home for my workshops and a personal haven for much of my writing for many years. This does not change the fact that my choice that weekend was a mistake, one that caused great pain for the man I was with and resulted in the loss of the opportunity for an ongoing friendship between us. I did feel guided by the magic and mystery of the interconnectedness of life to what became an important relationship and place in my life. But many other decisions I have made have not resulted in the unfolding of clearly fortunate events. And surely the Divine, if it does work with purpose in our lives, is not dependent upon but works through our choices, good and bad.

Maintaining that there are no mistakes, that "all things work out for the best," assumes a perspective that is wider, deeper, and longer than any to which we, as human beings, have access. It may well be true—although I cannot see how it could be argued that "things worked out for the best" for six million Jews in World War II. Such a position denies or glibly dismisses as necessary the very real and avoidable suffering that happens as a result of human failure. Worse, it suggests that we are not fully responsible for our choices because things are somehow predetermined. While this may be momentarily comforting, we simply have no way of knowing that it is true. I acknowledge and am often awed by the mystery that always holds and often guides me. This does not mean that I do not make mistakes, that I cannot fail.

Refusing to acknowledge failure is often an attempt to avoid the paralysis of shame. Many of us were raised or educated by people who tried to make us feel guilty when we made a mistake, hoping that fear of being shamed would help us avoid future failure. It didn't work. We cannot live fully and avoid mistakes. So, to avoid the paralysis and pain of shame, we narrow our lives to those things we already know and deny the mistakes that happen.

I was amazed to find how deeply rooted in me was this fear of the shame of failure. When my elder son, Brendan, was having difficulty in high school, going to the library to read instead of attending classes, because he was bored (you see—I want you to know I didn't fail to have a brilliant child; I just failed to have one who could endure the plodding rigors of the public school system), I was amazed at the terror I felt when it became apparent that he might fail a grade. All the nightmare associations from my school days came to the fore: people who fail a grade drop out, are unemployable, and die on the streets; those who fail a grade are marked for life as lacking, unworthy, unacceptable—shamed!

It is amazing how strong these fears are within me, even though I can now see that they are unfounded. How many times since you have become an adult has someone asked you what mark you received in ninth-grade geography? Even now, when I am anxious about something—anything—the most common dream I have is of being back in school, about to take an exam as I realize that I have not attended classes or studied. This, despite the fact that I have never come close to failing an exam in my life. And there was my son, not attending classes or studying, living out my worst nightmare.

When I tell others about my fear of failure, my own as a mother or my son's in school, I learn things I have not known about those close to me. One friend tells me she never got her degree because she just could not pass a statistics course. Another, as a young woman, had been pushed to perform music in front of an audience and was mortified when she wet her pants on stage. One after the other, people I respect and admire share their stories of failure with me. Amazingly, many of the most competent and caring adults I know failed or quit high school.

When we cannot live with failure, we limit the intimacy in our lives. People do not tell stories of failure to those who have room in their hearts only for perfection. Tell me a story of failure in your life, a time when you made a mistake. Tell it with compassion for the child or man or woman you were. Tell it with ruthless honesty and gentle acceptance. We do not avoid shame by hiding mistakes. The shame just becomes buried within us.

Shame releases its paralyzing grip on us when we take responsibility for our mistakes and the sometimes serious consequences those mistakes can have for ourselves and others. In this way shame can be our ally, pointing to things we have not accepted about ourselves, guiding us to mistakes we have not acknowledged. Accepting our failings means accepting where we have hurt others, or ourselves, and making retribution for these injuries where it is possible.

Accepting responsibility without falling into shame or blame is a tricky business. My failure to see and accept my physical limitations resulted in a long and debilitating illness. I burned out my immune system with too much doing, working, trying, and worrying. For years I fought this knowledge and consequently continued to make the mistakes that perpetuated the illness. It seemed easier for me to deal with the frustration and pain of illness than to take responsibility for my mistakes.

It was not until I was willing to look at what was, without judgment, that I could risk seeing and therefore be able to stop repeating my mistakes. I realized that while I am very good at esti-mating how much time it takes to do something—which is why I am seldom late—I am very bad at evaluating how much energy it takes to do something. If I can fit it into a time schedule, I think I can do it. After years of trying to change my inability—because I saw it as a moral failure not to be able to evaluate how much I could do—I now accept this about myself and compensate for it. I plan what I am going to do, and, knowing I have a kind of perceptual handicap about what my body, mind, and heart can accomplish in any given time, I arbitrarily reduce my plans by 30 to 50 percent. Or I run them by friends who have a much better sense of what is hu-manly possible, and I take their advice.

I live with the consequences of failing to recognize my mis-takes for years. My health is good, but my immune system is less than robust after so many years of being burned out. It may never fully re-cover. And, of course, there are factors that affect my health over which I have no immediate control—genetics, the quality of air and water I take in, the presence of infectious diseases around me.

I was not the only one to feel the consequences of my fail-ure to accept my physical limitations. My lack of energy and frequent illness have profoundly affected my children. It is hard to live with the knowledge of how our mistakes affect those we love, particularly those who are dependent upon us, who do not have the choice to walk away from us. The mistakes I have made with my sons, the fail-ures of mothering, are the hardest to live with. When someone tells me how wonderful these two young men are, I remember all the times I have shouted at them for unimportant things, all the times I have failed to be there with them fully. They are wonderful young men, but knowing how many mistakes I have made, I am sure they are wonderful not because of but in spite of my mistakes. But the question is, can I live with my failures and still say "Yes!" to life, still feel I deserve and am able to receive the beauty that is around me—including the beauty in the men my sons have become?

Forgiveness happens with time, as we learn to live with what cannot be changed. The capacity to live with what is hard is within us. When we can live consciously with the knowledge of what we or others have done, we are freed from the constant, if unconscious, effort of trying to pull away from what is. Trying to deny the mistakes we have made is like trying not to let your skin touch the cloth of a cold, wet jacket you are wearing—impossible, and exhausting in the trying.

We are afraid that our failures will mean that we will not be loved. But we don't earn love. How we treat others does, of course, affect our relationships. I do not want to be near the man who beat me. I do not trust the friend who has repeatedly lied to me. But we are loved for who we are, not for what we do. Love is larger than what we do. Love moves through us, if we let it.

One day I realized that I could love someone and still decide to separate myself from them if our behavior together was repeatedly damaging to each other. I did not have to try to stop loving him. And if I love another for who she is, not because she earns my love with her actions, then the same must also be true for those who love me. This isn't a license to treat those who love us badly, but it helps us step off the endless treadmill of doing for others, trying to be what we think they want us to be, in an attempt to earn their love. It doesn't work: we can't earn love.

At the end of the day, the failure I find the hardest to live with is the one that I made because I lacked the courage to let love take me where it will. And this mistake cannot be corrected by trying harder. It requires that I surrender to that which is larger than myself, that I be willing to move ahead where I am afraid of making mistakes. It requires telling the truth about my worst failures and saying, when I have no faith that anyone or anything is listening, "I don't know how to live with this, how to forgive myself. I cannot do this with my will. Help me."

In this place I sit and wait for love to find me, to come and take me home to the place where I—mistakes included—will be welcomed.

MEDITATION ON FORGIVENESS

Sit or lie down in a comfortable position and bring your attention to your breath. Follow the inhalation and exhalation, be aware of the rising and falling of your belly with the breath. If thoughts come, let them drift away effortlessly with the exhalation, and bring your attention back to your breath. Let any tiredness in your body melt away with the exhalation. Breathe into places of tension in your body, and feel the hardness yield to the softness of your breath, as the rocks yield to wind and water.

Now, think of a mistake you have made—start with a small error, a failure in judgment or resolve that did not have serious consequences. Remember the circumstances and feelings around the incident. See yourself as you were, and breathe the image of yourself into the center of your chest, placing the self that has made the mistake, that has failed, in your heart. You may want to focus on three or four times you have made a mistake, letting each image be about a more serious failure, a time when the consequences for yourself or others were more dire. Each time, breathe into your chest and feel your heart expand, creating room to hold each failure, each part of yourself that made a mistake.

Think now of others who have failed you in some way, others who have made mistakes that have had negative consequences for your life. Begin with someone you love who unintentionally caused a relatively minor consequence. See them making the mistake. Feel how your hurt and anger may have made you try, or want to try, to put them out of your heart. Breathe into your chest and feel your heart expand. Feel how there is limitless room there, in your heart, for all aspects of self and the world, and breathe back into your heart the one who has harmed you in some way. You may want to do this with those whose actions have had more serious consequences in your life, or with strangers who have offended you in some way.

In this meditation, do not push. Do not put the hurt part of yourself out of your heart in order to bring in someone or some part of yourself that has hurt you. If it feels difficult, simply sit with this feeling, without judgment, and feel the tension of wanting to put yourself or another out of your heart and simultaneously wanting to bring yourself or the other back into your heart. This does not require that you condone the mistakes made, only that you be willing to both live with what is and not put any aspect of yourself or the other out of your heart.

The Commitment

It doesn't interest me
to know where you live or how much money you have.
I want to know if you can get up,
after the night of grief and despair,
weary and bruised to the bone,
and do what needs to be done
to feed the children.

TRY THIS ONE MORNING as you are lying in bed: imagine millions of men and women all around the world rising from their beds where the sun finds them—leaving back-supporting mattresses and straw pallets, hammocks, futons, and thin blankets on dirt floors—to take care of the children. Regardless of their religion, culture, or material circumstances, there are noses to be wiped, bellies to be fed, tears to be dried, and answers to be provided for the questions of young minds. In modern cities and remote villages, luxurious mansions and desolate refugee camps, fires are lit, stoves are turned on, cereal boxes are opened, water is drawn from taps or pumps or streams, fruit is peeled, and breasts are bared for hungry mouths. It doesn't matter whether the men and women have the resources to adequately provide what the children need, or whether they feel like getting up and doing what has to be done—life cries out in its need to continue whether the providers are ill or healthy, illiterate or educated, despairing or filled with enthusiasm for life.

Reach out one morning with your imagination and feel them, the millions of men and women who do the best they can every day to feed their children's bodies, hearts, and minds.

My father was a lineman. He climbed hydro poles in northern Ontario, part of a team that made sure our small, remote community got the electrical power upon which much of our life depended. He started working when he was seventeen and retired when he was fifty-five. For thirty-eight years he left the house at 7:45 in the morning. At other times he would rise in the dark of the night and go out, through snow and temperatures well below zero, to restore power. The very rare occasion when he did not go when expected—I can remember only a couple of times that he stayed home ill with the flu for a day—made me uneasy as a child. I thought my father, this man who came home each evening smelling of creosote and sweat, sliding his metal lunch pail across the kitchen linoleum with a loud rattle, laughing and lifting me in his arms, was the strongest man on earth, a man capable of doing whatever was needed to provide for and protect us no matter what. Because he did. And he did it because he loved us, because he valued family in a way that people often do when they grow up without a happy family and longing for one; because it needed to be done.

When he was not working we spent a lot of time together—my mother, father, brother, and I—camping, fishing, hiking, playing broomball on the ice rink he built for us in the backyard. We went to church each Sunday and had dinner together every evening, after which we would read a small Bible passage and devotional piece, which we would discuss. It was these discussions that I loved the most; I examined and questioned every assumption of the beliefs I was being taught. If we were giving God credit for the Rousseau boy being pulled from the river when he fell through the ice last week, why couldn't we blame God if he had drowned? Why would a loving God insist that his son suffer and die on the cross for our sins? And how did that work exactly—how did Christ's death and resurrection actually "pay" for our sins? For that matter, what made something a sin?

In retrospect, I'm not sure anyone else at the dinner table enjoyed these theological musings like I did. But my parents' tolerance for and responses to my constant questions planted within me ideas that grew as I did: I learned that it is good to question even those concepts accepted by others as sacred, to think for myself; that there are no easy answers; that we always have a choice and we are responsible for our choices. These ideas, and the worlds they led me to, fed me as surely as the mashed potatoes and pork chops provided for my meal.

My mother was a homemaker. I am less certain about my mother's happiness with the life she chose, although she expresses no regrets and remains a vital, joyful woman. Perhaps I simply cannot separate my preferences from hers as easily as I can from my father's. She is a relentless organizer, fast thinker, and ruthless perfectionist, and I am not sure that looking after a family of four ever allowed her to fully use her talents. She lived according to what she valued—the traditional nuclear family and home. Pregnant with me at eighteen and married shortly thereafter in the mid-1950s, she probably never had much of a chance to discover what else she might have loved. If this is so, it only increases my admiration for how she did what needed to be done. She rose every morning before my father and made his breakfast and then ours. I don't remember her ever failing to do this or a thousand other daily tasks. If I saw my father as strong, my mother was invincible, someone who could be relied upon without thinking, like the rising of the sun or the solidity of the ground beneath my feet.

Full of vitality, my mother was always in motion, and she was not infrequently impatient with the demands and slowness of small children. My brother and I knew her temper and tried not to provoke it. But when I was very young I would wake up at night, not really needing anything, only wanting, in the darkness, to know my mother was there. I would lie in bed, debating whether or not to call to her. Finally, I would decide to call very softly, reasoning that if she was asleep she wouldn't hear me and if she was awake already she wouldn't be angry. No matter how quietly I called, she always appeared instantly at my bed, never impatient or angry. I would ask for a drink of water—she must have known it was a ruse—and she would bring me a glass and sit on the side of my bed for a few minutes, kiss me good night, and tell me she loved me. I remember the sweetness of knowing that no matter how softly I called she would always be there, and she would never be angry that I had called.

My parents did their best to feed their children's bodies, minds, and hearts, every day, whether they felt like it or not. Now that I have had children, I am in awe of how consistently they did this at such a young age, without complaint. They made a commitment to each other and to my brother and myself, and they kept it. I do not know what this cost them. I may never know. But having had children of my own, I know how hard it is some days to do what has to be done.

Many of my parents' generation were raised with a belief that was both curse and blessing: commitments were to be fulfilled, duties carried out. There was no choice. When we are convinced there is no choice, we waste less energy on wondering what to do and railing against that which needs to be done. This is the blessing we have when the rules are clear, the duties delineated. But there is another side to the ease we feel when our duty is laid out for us. If the strict parameters of what is expected do not fit us, we must shape ourselves to meet them, regardless of the costs. My mother, if she did not by nature fit the role of full-time homemaker, successfully managed the Herculean task of bending to meet it, without losing her enthusiasm for life, her ability to experience joy. Other women and their children were not so fortunate. Behind closed doors, within spotless rooms, many of my friends' mothers drowned the pain of not living who they were with alcohol and prescription drugs, and they sometimes descended into illness and suicide.

Many of the women of my generation are torn apart daily by the choices available to us, choices I am nevertheless grateful to have. When I went to work, I felt worried and guilty about leaving my children at day care. When I stayed home, I thought I would go out of my mind with the mental boredom, the struggle to live without enough money, and the worry that I would never be able to go back into the workplace and make a living. I had inherited my parents' values in a world with many more choices and demands, plus my own expectations that I could, and should, develop my own interests and talents. So, I tried to do it all—to keep a house and care for my children according to standards required of a full-time homemaker, to attend classes to develop my skills, and to work to provide money and financial security. And I got sick—very, very sick.

One of the gifts of lying on the floor too ill to get up with two young children to look after is the ease and clarity with which you know what really does have to be done. Now, when I work with men and women who are worn out with too much work and worry, who tell me all the things they *have* to do, I tell them, "You know, very little actually *has* to be done." I found out when I was ill that cookies do not *have* to be baked, floors do not *have* to be spotless, PTA meetings do not *have* to be attended, the dish drainer does not *have* to be emptied, meals do not *have* to be exotic and innovative. Too ill to do anything that did not have to be done, I did the impossible: I lowered my standards.

And then I did only what truly had to be done to feed the children. I made sure they were reasonably clean and dry and well fed. I listened to them and let them know they were loved. I stopped trying to find a place where there would be no tension between my desire to work in the world and my dedication to my children. I started to look for and find a way to simply live with this tension, holding it without struggle or hope of resolution.

In the ongoing sorting of what really did feed my children, I had to accept who I was. In some places I could and did stretch, but I also had to accept my limitations and not try to give my children something I simply did not have to give because I thought I *should* be able to. Sometimes they were the ones to teach me what I could and could not offer them.

When Nathan turned five, he had a birthday party—six small boys racing throughout the house at high speed and volume for four hours. I tried to be patient. I bought all the right things for the goodie bags, set up pin-the-tail-on-the-donkey, blew up balloons, and baked a cake. I wanted to be able to do it. And I hated it. Several days after the party, Nathan came and solicitously put his small hand on my arm as I sat at the kitchen table. "Mum," he said, "you're not good at parties. I had a good time but I think from now on Dad should do the parties. He doesn't mind what boys do so much. It's okay. You're good at other things. But you're not good at parties."

Nathan could see and accept who I was more easily than I could. And eventually, most days, I learned to accept that all that I can really offer my sons is who I am. I learned to stop trying to be someone else, to trust that what I could offer them would be enough, would feed them. So, I offered them the things I know and love: poetry, ideas, prayer, and time in the wilderness.

But the fact remains that there are things that children need, things that feed their bodies, hearts, and minds, that we may not feel up to providing some days. As creative as we can be about finding ways to provide these essential things while being all of who we are, there are some days when we must simply draw on something deep within us and do what has to be done, even though we do not want to or think we can. I once had a teacher who was very keen on always being "at cause"—being the sole determiner of one's own actions—and never being "at the effect"—having one's actions directed or curtailed by circumstances or the needs and wants of others. The first time I met him I asked, in all innocence, "How can I be 'at cause' at three o'clock in the morning when one of my sons is ill and I have to get up and look after him?"

He had no answer for me and told me that this was why he disliked children so much—because they were so needy. It was looking after my sons that taught me the answer to my question.

When Brendan was small and waking up at night to nurse, I worried about how long it would go on. I would jerk myself awake and anxiously watch him for reassurance that he would go right back to sleep, silently begging him to do so. I was completely at "the effect" of the demands of mothering. Brendan's needs were determining my actions, and it was wearing me out.

When Nathan was born, I did not have the anxiety of the first-time mother. I knew that no matter how often or for how long he got up at night, eventually he would sleep through. After all, how many eighteen-year-olds do you know who need their mothers during the night? (Okay, but how many do you know who actually want them to appear?) It had passed with Brendan—it would pass with Nathan. This knowledge helped me surrender to what had to be done. Instead of fighting it, worrying about it, adding the suffering of anxiety to the discomfort of sleeplessness, I surrendered to the task in front of me. Although Nathan got up more often than Brendan, it was less tiring to feed him, and, probably because he did not pick up my tension, he went directly back to sleep much more often.

In a culture that values individual freedom over all else, this is what we too often have lost, what we must remember if we are to do what has to be done for the future of our people without sacrificing our souls: how to surrender to doing what needs to be done to feed the minds and bodies and hearts of our children. And who are not our children? When we surrender, when we do not fight with life when she calls upon us, we are lifted, and the strength to do what needs to be done finds us.

It is easy to forget this, especially when we are weary and bruised through the center of our being by life's disappointments, by illness or poverty or grief. And it is there, in that moment when it seems impossible, when we think we have nothing more to draw upon, that something else can enter, if we surrender to the tasks life demands of us. In this place, there is no more trying. There is only being and doing what needs to be done. We are "at cause" because we have remembered that we can choose to serve the only cause that matters: life herself. And in our capacity to do this willingly, when we get up anyway and do what needs to be done for love, we shine with dignity. When I see this in another I am filled with an infinite tenderness for our fragility and our strength.

I want to be with those who know of this, who have met within themselves the ability to feed the children when they thought they could not. These are the men and women who have, with great humility, tasted their own nobility.

MEDITATION FOR THOSE WHO FEED THE CHILDREN
Sit or lie down in a comfortable position and bring your attention to your breath. Follow each inhalation and exhalation in and out of your body. Let your belly become very soft, and allow any hardness or tension or tiredness to melt away with each exhalation. Let go of all the trying held in your body.

Now, let your imagination bring to you the reality of millions of men and women who take care of the children every day. Reach out with your mind's eye and see them: mothers rising in the early morning and dressing sleepy young children, fathers carrying small tired ones home to bed; strong arms rocking small bodies; men and women driving or walking to factories and offices and fields to provide for their children . . . See what images come to you. Feel how, despite the differences of culture and place, the desire to care for the children and the willingness to do what is needed are so much the same. Say a prayer for these men and women and their small charges; surround them with a light of strength and peace and gratitude, that they may have what they need to care for the children.

Remember now who cared for you. Bring your attention back to your breath and wait for the images that will come. Even if your childhood was hard, someone cared for you, fed you, saw you, and touched you, if only intermittently. It may have been a parent or a teacher, an aunt or uncle, or a family friend. Remember the times when your body or heart or soul was fed, and say a prayer of thanks to those who fed you. Let your heart remember what you received and be filled with gratitude.

Follow your breath, and turn your attention now to those who are afraid that they will not be able to feed their children: those in refugee camps and places of war who are watching their children slowly starve to death; the mothers who wait for their sons to come home in the big city ghettos, afraid for their lives in these places of violence; those who have no access to schools or hospitals to ensure their children's minds and bodies will flourish. Feel their dreams for their children, feel how these dreams are the same as those of all who dream for the children they love. Feel their desperation, and how, with great courage, they do what they can. Say a prayer for these men and women and their children; surround them with a rainbow of love and strength.

Bring your attention back to your breath and your own life. What in your life feeds the children? See how, in the way you go about your daily life, the way you are with others, the way you care for your home, your community, and the earth, you have an opportunity to contribute to what needs to be done to feed the children. Be aware of how everyone is, at times, a child—innocent, in need of care, deserving of tenderness. Be aware of the nonhuman children of this planet: the animals, plants, and minerals, the air and the water. If you want to, choose to, breathe out your "yes," your willingness to do what is needed, to feed all the children, to care for the world.

The Fire

It doesn't interest me who you know
or how you came to be here.
I want to know if you will stand
in the center of the fire
with me
and not shrink back.

SOMETIMES WE GO OUT AND SEEK the fire that will burn away what is dross in our lives. More often, we awaken suddenly to find ourselves encircled by flame. Intense experiences of the heart transform us. I want to know if you can stand with me, eyes wide open, when the fire—asked for or unbidden—consumes all we think we know. I want to know if you will offer yourself as fuel for the flames and let the Mystery we seek, the Divine we long for, which comes in unpredictable ways, consume and transform you.

Talking about the fire, we forget what it is really like. It is only in the stories of our burning and rising from the ashes that we remember the flame.

Five years ago in my kitchen, as I stood talking with my friend, everything was as it had been, more or less, for thirty-eight years. And in one moment, as she raised a hand to the right side of her head and complained of a sudden headache, everything changed. That is what it is like: after the fire, nothing is ever the same again.

Remembering, I see the scenes in slow motion, without sound but in vivid color. I see myself, as if viewing a stranger, moving across the black-and-white floor tiles, my forehead creased with concern, putting an arm around Catherine, moving her toward a chair. My arm feels inadequately slender around her solid body. There is no evidence that something is seriously wrong, but I am suddenly certain we must get to a hospital.

I see us walking down the front steps of my house, Catherine getting into the front seat of my small red car parked at the curb. She complains of nausea so I hand her a green plastic mixing bowl, which she carefully places on her lap after fastening her seat belt.

I can hear the seat belt click. I cannot hear the children laughing on the sidewalk in the late-afternoon sun as we drive down the street, but I notice them on the periphery of my vision, running, tossing a ball. I see myself driving, Catherine vomiting into the plastic bowl. I keep driving. The bowl tumbles to the floor of the car in a slow-motion cascade as Catherine convulses, once, twice. Her eyes roll back, her body strains against the seat belt that holds her in place, and she becomes, finally, still, her head hanging forward, swinging with the motion of the car, her body slumped, lifeless.

It's like watching a movie with the sound track turned off. For a moment I do not recognize the driver of the car. Her face, my face, has become unfamiliar with fear. Her mouth, my mouth, opens. I hear no sound but see the shape of two words: "Catherine! No!"

What happens next is harder to see, the memories disjointed sensations, broken thoughts. I know she is dead. I reject this information. I know the hospital is five minutes away. I know five minutes will be too late. As I continue driving, my attention splits and I feel as if I am reaching up, straining toward the sky. There is a wrenching sensation of muscles being pulled away from the bone and then a feeling of being catapulted out of the car. Suddenly I can see the roof of the car, the tops of the trees along the street, fresh green in the spring warmth, and above me something glimmering, like a long, silver, liquid balloon drifting toward the clouds, the string dangling. I lunge for it, grab it, and pull down.

My body jerks with a violent shiver, a sensation similar to the jolt that sometimes pulls me back from the threshold of sleep as I drift off at night. My hands ache where they are gripping the steering wheel. I am aware once again of the street before me and Catherine's body hanging on the seat belt, rising and falling now with her breath. Needing to hear the sound of my own voice, I tell her to keep breathing, to hang on. I try to swallow and cannot. A voice whispers, "If you panic now she is dead." For the first time in my life, I have an overwhelming desire to scream.

As I drive I keep holding on, wrapping myself around the shining filament I have pulled down from the sky and anchoring it there, in the soft, round body beside me. I will not let go. My own breath is ragged. My arms quiver slightly with fatigue.

A silent prayer comes without thought: "Help me. I'll never get her to the hospital like this. Please, help me."

We are approaching the end of the block. It has been no more than two minutes since we walked to the car. As we near the intersection I hear a voice, quiet and calm: "Drive into the intersection and lean on the horn." I do not hesitate at the stop sign but drive blindly into the intersection, horn blasting. A police car coming along the street to my left screeches to a halt next to us.

Things speed up. An ambulance arrives. Twice on the way to the hospital, Catherine is resuscitated. The surgeon at first refuses to operate. The damage from the aneurysm is too great. He is sure she will not live or, if she does, she will have no brain function. A compact, efficient man with silver hair, he is matter-of-fact in his assessment.

I wait. I hang on. Alone at her bedside after the doctor has left, I hold her hand and speak softly, fervently, "You can come back, Catherine. It doesn't matter what you hear them say. You can come back to your life, completely, fully recovered if you want to." I believe this to be true. Hours pass. Roger, her husband, arrives. The doctors operate to stop the bleeding, and Catherine slips into a coma.

We sit in the intensive-care unit beside her comatose form, wires and tubes and monitors flashing. After five weeks, the chaplain begins to talk of taking her off the respirator, of letting her die. Roger asks me what I think he should do, and I go off to sit alone in the park.

The park is a busy place, full of winos, squirrels, and pigeons. I find a spot under one of the largest maple trees, and there I let the sounds of the city rise and fall around me as I find and follow the rhythm of my breath, closing my eyes and waiting for my thoughts to drift away. There was a time when I would have been afraid to sit so open and relaxed in a downtown park, but these are fearless days. I have seen how fast everything can change. There is no time to waste on fearing what might happen. The scavengers of the park must sense my lack of vulnerability. None approach; they leave me to my solitude.

It doesn't take long. For five weeks I have kept one part of my attention linked to Catherine wherever I am. I find the stillness easily and call to her now, seeing her smiling before me.

Catherine has been my student for five years, coming to participate in workshops, often assisting with the cooking and cleaning. I sat at her bedside and held her hand after her two miscarriages. She brought me juice and warm muffins in the morning when I was ill. Sitting on my great-grandmother's quilt sipping tea, we told each other our night dreams. I love her. She trusts me.

She looks at me now in my mind's eye and arches her eyebrows in a familiar gesture of inquiry. "They're thinking of turning off the respirator, Catherine. Roger has to give them a decision." Her face becomes serious, thoughtful. "What do you want to do?" I ask.

She hesitates. "I need twenty-four hours," she says. I nod, blink, and open my eyes to the blinding sunlight bouncing off the sidewalk.

Roger tells the chaplain he will make a decision in twenty-four hours. Eighteen hours later, Catherine comes out of the coma, and for one moment more I allow myself to imagine that everything has not been changed, that what we thought we knew has remained intact.

The respirator tube comes out and Catherine regains her voice. She recognizes me and her mother but asks me to identify the man in the picture beside her bed. It is her husband, Roger. While she remembers all of the prayers and songs we have learned together, she does not know how to use a toothbrush or a spoon. She seems strangely detached from what has happened to her; her emotional affect is flat. Over time, bits and pieces are found and woven back into the fabric of memory and daily functioning, but it remains a patchwork quilt with some squares missing, and others reappearing unpredictably only to vanish again. Today, five years after the surgery, she remains physically and mentally handicapped. She needs care twenty-four hours a day.

She is changed forever. And so am I. When Catherine's brain aneurysm burst, all I had learned, all I had worked for, was on the line. And it wasn't enough. I wanted to save her, to restore her to what she was. What incredible arrogance! What amazing innocence. A hero's skills and courage could not do what was needed. I was confronted with the illusion of my belief that I could make things right when it really mattered, if I simply tried hard enough. I couldn't. And if all of my work could not ensure some basic immunity from tragedy for those I loved, then what was the point of what I was learning and teaching? Why was I working so hard?

To continue, I had to live differently. I had to find the ability to live with the vastness of what I do not know and what I cannot control. I don't know whether I did the right thing, reaching for Catherine and pulling her back. I don't know if in fact that is what I did, although Catherine's account of what happened coincides with my experience of doing just that. I doubt that I would do it differently if I could do it all again, even though I have often thought it would have been easier for Catherine and those who love her—

easier for me—if she had died. I do not know why she chose to come back. I don't know if she really had a choice, although she feels she did.

Standing in the center of the fire with Catherine changed me. I developed a level of ruthless honesty and an almost physical aversion to the small daily lies we sometimes tell ourselves. If life is precious and fragile, I do not want to waste one moment on polite half-truths. So, when a student I care about, weeping and broken, tells me that she cannot imagine how her husband of eighteen years could have lied to her so consistently during their marriage, that it is not in her to understand this kind of subterfuge, I tell her, as gently as I can, "Of course you can, because you also lied for eighteen years—to yourself. You abandoned yourself and pretended not to see the truth. That's the hard part."

I could not save Catherine. All I could do was refuse to close my eyes and my heart as the fire surrounded us both, refuse to soften the edges with comforting explanations—whether of God's plan or karmic lessons—I could not know to be true. Sometimes this is the only choice we have—to refuse or agree to stay awake as we are torn open by what is beyond our control. And I found that I can do it, if I choose to—I can stay awake and let the sorrows of the world tear me apart and then allow the joys to put me back together, different from before but whole once again.

Tell me about the fires of transformation that have swept through your life. Were you alone or did you have a friend, someone who loved you, there by your side with her eyes wide open, gripping your hand in hers?

Catherine's refusal to let go of my hand when the fire surrounded us sustained me and challenged all I thought I knew.

A year after coming out of the coma, Catherine attends a
women's retreat I am leading at a wilderness campsite. Sitting
propped up on an inflated mattress set on the ground, listing a little
to the side that is partially paralyzed, Catherine is surrounded by
cedars and hemlocks and the sounds of a dozen women talking and
laughing as they gather and cut firewood. Her close-fitting cap, the
kind with ear flaps, sits slightly askew, exposing the place on her
forehead where the bone is sunken, a round indentation about the
size of a dollar coin.

Everything she does takes great concentration. Periodically,
one of the women carrying wood hands her a small branch. Slowly,
laboriously, she breaks off twigs and stacks them on the ground beside her legs. She has been doing this for over an hour. The pile of
broken sticks is about three inches high. She wants to help, to participate in the wood gathering.

I stop for a moment to watch her. She looks up and smiles
at me. I try to smile back, to breathe past the ache in my chest
that comes whenever I watch her. I go over to sit on the ground
beside her.

There is a politeness, a formality in Catherine's speech that
was not there before. It creates a strange distance between us. Since
she came out of the coma, her tone has been consistently without
emotion. I have not seen her cry.

Suddenly, she reaches for my hand with her own and leans
toward me. "I want to thank you for making it possible for me to

be here." I try to smile, my throat closing. "I want you to know, I know I wouldn't be here at all, alive, if it wasn't for you."

I try to rub the ache in my chest away with the heel of my hand, shrugging with a feigned casualness and forcing my voice to sound matter-of-fact. "You chose to live, Catherine."

"Yes." Her voice is very soft, as if she is trying not to startle me. "I did. But you gave me that choice. I was so scared, so confused, and you reached out and grabbed me and held me. You stayed right there with me, through all those days and nights."

The forbidden words come out in a rush. "I sometimes wonder if I did you any favor."

She squeezes my hand. "I know it must be hard for you to watch your friend. But no matter how hard it seems or how much she struggles, she has never regretted coming back. She is glad to be alive and wants you to know this."

Her reference to herself in the third person is disorienting. She often mixes her pronouns, but this is different. It is as if she is speaking to me of the Catherine I knew before, as if the woman she was is still there, silent, unseen. I want to talk to that woman, to the Catherine I knew, for just one minute, to tell her how much I love her. I just want one minute with her to say good-bye.

She watches me closely. "Life is still good." I want to believe her. But how is it still good, this life she has? "I've learned a lot." Her voice is small, almost tentative.

"Really?" I ask. A sucker for learning, I reach for something that would make it all worthwhile. "What?"

"Well . . ." she mulls, "I've learned to live fully in the present." She lets out a short laugh. "It's all I've got. I can't remember what just happened or what's planned next."

She pauses and looks out over the lake, her own eyes for the first time full of tears. Her voice is hoarse. She speaks very slowly. "And I've learned that really bad things can happen to me." I put my arm around her. She leans her scarred forehead against mine. Silent tears slide down our cheeks.

Suddenly, the long, eerie call of a loon splits the silence and echoes off the lake as three of the birds land on the water in front of us, two males and one female. All the women working in the clearing pause to watch them.

"Where is his mate?" Catherine asks, referring to the extra male. Adult loons mate for life and are generally seen in pairs.

"They left here together last fall, but he returned alone in the spring," I tell her. "She must have died on the journey." The loon opens his bill and sends out his lonely call across the lake as if to confirm my story.

"He will be alone now, then." Catherine's voice is once again slow and emotionless.

"Yes," I answer, "he will be alone."

We sit quietly and watch the birds swim across the lake, the late-afternoon sun sparkling on the water, the smell of cedar and wood smoke mingling with the first hint of autumn in the air. The loons call to one another, their intermittent song strangely mournful and yet hauntingly beautiful. It is a sound that always makes me feel like I am being beckoned, called home, reminded of something or some place I thought I could never forget. After a few moments, Catherine turns to me and squeezes my hand, her eyes bright, her face open and smiling. "Is this not the most beautiful place, this earth we live on?"

I cannot help but smile back. "Yes, Catherine. Yes, it is."

MEDITATION FOR OPENING THE HEART

When the chaos of fire surrounds and consumes us, it is difficult to keep our hearts open, to feel the fear and pain. This adaptation of a Sufi meditation helps us to find the stillness in the midst of chaos, gives us a way to find and open our hearts. It is there, in the strong, soft center of the heart, that we find the courage and the willingness to stand in the center of the fire. When we are connected to our hearts, we can hear the small voice that says with quiet confidence, "Breathe. You can do this."

Sit or lie down in a comfortable position. Bring your attention to your breath. Take three large breaths in through your nose and exhale out through your mouth, letting your body relax and your muscles release with each exhalation. Breathe into your heart and let the muscles around your heart release. Let your breath dissolve any hardness here with its softness.

Now, on each exhalation, with your mouth closed, make the sound "hmmmm . . ." three times. Inhale and repeat this sound with the exhalation for a total of twenty-two breaths, making the sound three times on each exhalation. The sound is more an inward than an outgoing sound. You should be able to feel it vibrating in your jaw and deep within your chest. Imagine your heart relaxing and opening a little more with each breath.

At the end of twenty-two breaths, sit in the silence for eleven breaths, letting your mind come to stillness in the inner quiet. Then, on a large breath, begin again to make the sound, three times on each exhalation, this time for eleven breaths. Again, feel the vibration of the sound in the center of your body and imagine your heart relaxing and opening. At the end of eleven breaths, sit in the silence and breathe in and out of your heart. Feel in your heart the courage, the willingness, to stand in the center of the fire without shrinking back.

Deep Sustenance

It doesn't interest me where or what or with whom
you have studied.
I want to know what sustains you,
from the inside,
when all else falls away.

TELL ME, HAVE YOU BEEN WHERE HOPE and faith cannot find you? What sustains you when all that you have relied upon, inner and outer, falls away? How do you get through? How do you take the next breath?

Most of the time, I am buoyed up by hope: I have hope that my sons will find what they love and a way to live it; I have hope that my work will continue to challenge me and offer something of value to others. Oh, I also have hope that we will use our will and imagination to bring peace to parts of the world torn by war and to develop technologies and ways of living that are in alignment with the earth. But the truth is that most of the time, the hopes that move me toward life with arms wide open are smaller, particular, and very human: I have hope that I will, someday, exercise on a regular basis; I have hope that I will once again feel the delicious excitement of falling in love; I have hope that my skin will clear up, I will learn how to roller blade gracefully, and I will be kissed again by a man who takes my breath away. I have hope that I will find the time today to walk by the lake and feed the ducks.

There is, of course, a risk in focusing on what we hope for—we can fall into the daydream, missing what we have. But our ability to imagine, to anticipate, is part of what makes us human. Anyone who has ever made love knows that part of the pleasure is in anticipating both the familiar and the unknown. The pleasure and intimacy of lovemaking are deepened when I am able to slow down and consciously savor the sharp taste of the moment in between, the second just before, the place where the breath catches in anticipation. I am aware of the scent of heat held in the air between two mouths reaching for each other hungrily. There is hope that sustains, that moves me toward life, in the skin that tingles, waiting, fine hairs at attention, reaching, aching. There is anticipation in the places that have not yet been touched but know they will be. There is hope of being fully met by the one who can touch me without taking his eyes from mine.

Hoping and anticipating can deepen our experience of the moment, motivate us to act or sit still. I do my daily meditation not only because it brings me insight and a sense of calmness as I do it, but because I have hope that it will enable me to be more present in my daily living. Living the present moment fully and having hope for what is to come next are not mutually exclusive. Sometimes, when the moment at hand is difficult, having hope that it will change is what makes it possible to be present.

And sometimes, there is no hope. When I am lying in bed, ill again after months of doing all I know to stay well, I feel no hope that I will ever have normal, daily health. When my son once again skips classes, I lose hope that he will find his way within the school system. Sometimes, when I ache with loneliness, I have no hope that I will find a partner with whom to share my life.

But there is still faith. Sometimes, when hope is gone, I can breathe into my heart and find there the faith that sustains me, faith that is fueled by the moments when I or others are able to find what is good, what is funny, sweet, and tender in life, despite deep wounds and overwhelming difficulties. It is the courage of the human spirit and the relentless persistence of life all around us that gives me faith. So I have faith that even if my health is never strong, even if my son continues to flounder in his schooling, even if I never come together with the husband of my heart and hearth—it will be okay, truly okay. Life will continue, and it will conspire with its beauty to pull me back to hope. This is my faith.

Living with hope is living with anticipation of what can be. Living with faith is relaxing into what is that cannot be changed by our will, and knowing that life in its fullness is good.

And sometimes, neither hope nor faith can find me and there is nothing to hang on to. When this happens, the late-night hours are the worst. I watch TV, work at my computer, or clean the house, wanting to exhaust myself so that when I stop I will fall into a dreamless sleep, bypassing the ache that leaves me staring blindly into the darkness.

In these moments, all that buoyed me up in more hopeful times seems colorless, flat, not worth the trouble. Food loses its taste. I take no pleasure in my home, which suddenly seems too familiar—just so much stuff arbitrarily collected and waiting for the garbage heap. My relationships with friends and family are suspect, and I long to disappear. The ideas that normally stimulate and excite me seem meaningless, remote from anything that matters—my writing, petty self-indulgence. My dreams are full of ambivalence: reluctant lovers, confused decisions, and endless tasks that leave me exhausted. At these times I have no faith, no knowledge that this too will pass, that who we are and how we live matters at all.

The times without faith and hope are sometimes brought about by loss. A number of years ago, over a period of about twenty months, one by one, many of the things in my life that gave me hope fell away or were threatened: my sons and I had to leave our home of twelve years; Catherine's brain aneurysm left me grieving, questioning my basic beliefs, and canceling my teaching plans; my younger son, Nathan, ill for weeks, was hospitalized as the doctors searched for a cause, suspecting cancer but finding nothing; my relationship with the man I thought I had waited for all my life ended; my closest friend learned she had cancer and decided to move away to seek healing; my sanctuary in the wilderness was devastated by a tornado while a group of us were camping there, leaving us shaken and the site looking clear-cut and barren.

As each of these things happened, I responded, as most would, by doing what had to be done. In many ways, it is not the time of crisis that is hardest to bear. I have learned how to be with a dying friend or a sick child, how to gather strength to pack boxes, paint walls, and repitch wind-torn tents. But later, when the crises were past, when there was nothing left to be done, I found myself sitting on my bed unable to sleep. After a long time, only two lines flowed from my pen onto the blank page of my journal. It was only as I read those lines that I realized how far I had wandered from hope and faith.

Too late, alone in my bed, I whispered slowly into the darkness, "I am not as tough as I look. I am not indestructible."

I didn't know, until I wrote those lines, that I'd thought I was invincible. But I had. I'd thought my faith and hopes would sustain me no matter what. I had been down and gotten up before— after failed marriages, illnesses, disappointments. I had thought I would always be able to get up. Now, for the first time in my life, I was not sure. I had no faith that this deep weariness would pass, that hope would ever find me again. My friends were concerned, but I felt a great distance from them, an unwillingness or inability to receive their support. Something inside me closed.

When all we have relied upon has fallen away, there is nothing to do but wait without faith or hope. How we wait—whether we remain open or close up—is the choice we have to make, a choice to either live or begin to spiral down toward death. To choose life we have to be willing to wait, open to life and love at a time when opening seems impossible and we are sure that no one and nothing will ever be able to find us.

What sustain us when all else falls away are the things that make waiting and staying open to life possible. I have been lucky enough to find three such things in my life—my practices of prayer and meditation, writing, and spending time close to nature. These activities enrich my life when I have hope and faith, and they give me a way to bear the waiting. What makes them practices is that I do them regularly, whether I feel like it or not.

A practice of any kind is best cultivated in times when things are going well. This is difficult for us. Sometimes any regular activity beyond daily teeth-brushing seems a curtailment of personal freedom. But a practice, a regularly repeated and at least minimally structured way of connecting with our sense of the Mystery of which we are a part, gives us a way to open to that which sustains us when everything falls away.

I began my practice very simply: I said a small prayer each morning to greet the day. Later I began, at the end of the day, to share prayers with my sons. We would each offer our thanks for something in the day, the names of those we loved for blessing, and any requests we had for help and guidance. Eventually, I began to do an hour of daily meditation and prayer. There is almost always some resistance—the voice that says I am too tired, too busy, too ill to do it, or healthy enough not to need it. And I do it anyway.

Most spiritual practices have been developed—and, in the past, were sustained—in community. But most of us do not live in community. Although my students and friends and I share many of these practices, we are only occasionally in proximity to one another. Doing a daily practice alone is difficult. It requires not so much a heroic discipline as a deep commitment to life, a willingness to dedicate our lives to something larger than ourselves.

I want to know what your life is dedicated to. What do you love more than your own happiness or your own pain? Each day, as

I do my practice, I dedicate my small life to being fully here, to learning how to love well.

And the practice I have cultivated in easier times is there when things are hard. I say the prayers I have been taught. They are the prayers of the Twisted Hair Council of Elders, but they could just as easily be the prayers of Tibetan Buddhism, of a Christian community, or of one of the many other spiritual traditions. When I am in despair, I can come up with no eloquent, spontaneous prayers, so I begin by rote. At such times I do not feel like saying these prayers. I have no hope that they will make a difference, no faith that there is anything receiving my words. My words are stark and blunt. I follow the structure I was taught, which, in easier times, I have articulated with passion and poetry.

At other times I walk along the shore of the great lake of fresh water near my home, sitting on the rocks and looking at it with unseeing eyes. What previously moved me with its beauty now seems cold and lifeless. But I walk along the shore anyway, and the sound of the waves begins to penetrate what has become hard inside me. And there are still other times when I let my pen move across the page, the words pouring from me, though they seem trite, empty, and meaningless. But I keep on writing. And as I pray, or watch the water, or keep my hand moving across the page, something inside me loosens—and I am aware once again of how I am held. It may take some time, and I may experience it for only a moment, but it is enough to help me go on.

Tell me, can you love life and let love find you when you are lost? What sustains you, what helps you sit without hope and wait, opening your heart to love when you have no faith that love exists? My practices are simply ways of picking up my end of the thread that links me to love and life, even when I have no hope or faith that the other end of the thread is connected. And every time—every single time—love finds me, sometimes in the impossible relief of experiencing once again the deep knowing that I am held, sometimes in the shiver of sweet ecstasy as I unexpectedly kiss the face of the Mystery, and sometimes in the warmth of being touched deeply by the words and actions of the people who reach out for me. It may take a moment or what feels like forever, but I am found and I can receive the touch of Spirit, of the world, of others—the touch that brings me back to life and hope.

When my friend Catherine was in a coma, I spent days waiting and praying. One day, going home from the hospital, as I drove out of the parking lot, the attendant smiled and asked me, "How are you today?"

I suppose it was my tiredness that made me answer truthfully. I just didn't have the energy to lie. "Horrible," I said bluntly. "I've just come from the hospital, where my friend is dying."

I wasn't expecting any kind of meaningful response. I waited for him to mutter something about it being too bad. But instead, he leaned out of his booth, his voice filled with genuine concern, and said, "I am so sorry. What happened to her?"

I told him. He told me that his mother had had a stroke the week before. The doctors didn't think she would recover. He gave me my change and I drove away feeling a little lighter, a little more connected where I had earlier felt cast adrift.

Four weeks later, with Catherine still in the coma, I again found myself driving out of the same parking lot. As I looked for money to pay the fee, I heard a warm voice: "How is your friend doing? Is she okay? Did she make it?" It was the same attendant, and somehow, in the busiest parking lot in a city of over two million, he had recognized me and remembered my story.

Our brief exchange affected me deeply. As I drove away, I felt an impossible sense of hope. This man's willingness to extend himself to a stranger sustained me in a way I could not have anticipated. My usual defenses of self-sufficiency, my wariness about receiving from someone I did not know, fearing something might be wanted in return, had been dissolved by weeks of stress and need. The truth is, I only have to receive and give what I am able. There is no risk. The intimacy, the interconnectedness of all life that is the love to which we all belong, can only be given and received. It cannot be taken.

And when it is given and received, we are sustained.

MEDITATION FOR WAITING

This basic body-scan meditation has perhaps been the most important part of the daily practice I use that helps me wait, without closing to life, when I have no faith or hope. Doing it on a regular basis when you are hopeful means you will be able to return to it more easily when you are visited by despair. The ability to simply be, to let go when you feel you are hanging on by your fingernails, can be enough sometimes to help you continue, to let you wait for that which sustains you to find you again.

Lie down on your back in a comfortable position. Bring you attention to your breath, feeling your belly rise on the inhalation and fall on the exhalation. With each exhalation, let go of any stress or tension or tiredness, letting it flow harmlessly into the floor and the earth beneath you. Let any thoughts or feelings that come drift away with the exhalation, and bring your attention gently back to your breath and your body.

Turn your attention now to your feet. Imagine being able to breathe into your feet, filling them with light and warmth. On the exhalation let any tension or tiredness in your feet flow harmlessly out into the ground, and feel your feet relax and soften. Let go of your feet.

Breathe into your legs, into the shin bones and calf muscles. Be aware of any tension or tiredness held here, and breathe it out. Breathe into your knees and your thighs, feeling their shape and weight, being aware of the long, strong bones that go from knee to hip. Let the thigh muscles soften, letting go of any tension or tiredness with the exhalation.

Breathe into your pelvis, being aware of your hip bones, your buttocks and genitals. Fill your pelvis with breath and light, and let go on the exhalation of any stress or tension or tiredness held there. Feel the pelvis soften and relax with the exhalation.

Breathe into your lower back, letting your breath come up your spine one vertebra at a time, gently bringing the bones into smooth alignment. Breathe into the muscles of your back, filling them with breath and exhaling all stress or tension or tiredness. Let the inhalation penetrate the places that are hard, bringing softness. Let go on the exhalation.

Breathe into your belly and up, into your chest, filling your lungs and heart with light and breath. Be aware of your rib cage rising and falling. Let the muscles around your heart relax. Breathe into any hardness and let it soften with the breath. Let all the tension and tiredness in the front of your body flow out with the exhalation.

Breathe into your hands—the fingers, the palms—and up into your arms and shoulders, filling them with light and warmth and exhaling out any stress or tension held there. Breathe into your throat and neck. Let a small sound come with the exhalation, releasing the hardness of unspoken words. Breathe into your face. Let your mouth open slightly, and feel your eyes sink a little. Feel the muscles of your forehead and your cheeks release any tension and tiredness with your exhalation. Breathe into your scalp and the bones of your head, feeling the exhalation carry with it any stress or tension or tiredness. Let go.

Be aware of your whole body. Breathe into any places that still hold tension or tiredness. Let go of the hardness of hanging on. Feel yourself being supported by the floor and the earth beneath the floor. Let go. Breathe.

Finding Our Way Home

I want to know if you can be alone
with yourself
and if you truly like the company you keep
in the empty moments.

TELL ME ABOUT A MOMENT of real solitude, a moment when you were with yourself and felt yourself at the center, a moment when you could feel the world, the stars, the galaxies spinning around you.

In the spring of 1974, I took the train home at the end of my college term. There was one train a day that left Toronto in the early evening and arrived in my hometown, four hundred miles north, at 4:30 in the morning. No one knew I was coming, so there was no one there to meet me at the station. The only person to get off the train, I stood for a moment on the wooden platform and then swung my knapsack onto my back and started to walk toward home. My family lived on the opposite side of town, about a mile and a half away.

It was dark when I started walking, but by the time I'd reached the bridge that spanned the river in the center of town, walking past stores and restaurants and the town's single traffic light, dutifully changing color although there was not a car in sight, the sky was streaked with the pink-gold of dawn, and the birds were singing the sun up.

It's the quiet I remember most, the sweet stillness of the whole town sleeping. I was nineteen—in blue jeans, denim jacket, and a yellow T-shirt, with long, straight, blonde hair. I inhaled a great gulp of the cool spring air and found myself smiling for no apparent reason. I suddenly realized that no one knew where I was. And yet I was there, close to so many who knew me. Walking down the center of the deserted streets, past the familiar houses, I felt invisible—seeing and yet not being seen, by choice. For the first time in my life I felt truly alone and completely with myself. I imagined the people I knew in those houses—sleeping, dreaming, waking to the growing light and rolling over to find one more hour of sleep—unaware that someone was walking past, observing their lives in motion.

I paused for a long time and watched the river. Endlessly muddy with the brown-red soil of the surrounding clay belt, the water flowed into the lake in an infinite stream whether I or anyone else was there to see it or not, just as the town and the life I had known growing up continued, whether I was miles away in the city or here, silently watching. Walking on, I passed a house as a light was turned on and a woman, wrapped in her bathrobe, moved past the kitchen window to fill a kettle and put it on the stove as she did every morning at this same time.

It was as if I had stepped outside something of which I had always, unconsciously, been a part and was seeing it for the first time—this stream of life, this cycle of ordinary living that goes on within and around us all the time. I knew that in a moment, when I went through my parents' door, I would become a part of it again and lose this acute sense of being the witness, alone and completely with myself and my own thoughts. I knew I would be swept up in the hugs and exclamations of surprise and greeting, the sharing of news and the sounds and smells of bacon and eggs and coffee—the irresistible tide of living in the world. But for this moment, I was with the world, watching it but somehow not in it. I was alone with myself.

I paused on the patio outside the back door, prolonging the moment. I was alone, lost to everyone and yet not lost but there, on the doorstep. I knew that home was as much in the slow walk alone through the quiet streets as it was in the arrival at this door. Home was in the taste of being with myself, walking next to what was familiar, toward what was cherished.

Then I opened the door, crossed the threshold with conscious deliberation, and called out, "Isn't anyone in here up yet?" As my mother came into the kitchen, I glanced back outside, and in my mind's eye I saw that other young woman standing there—backpack on, watching us and grinning at me. I knew I would get back to her. I had met myself walking home in the dawn, and I liked the company I'd kept in those empty moments.

Tell me, have you met yourself? Have you been able to step outside the business of life for just one moment and look in from the outside, feeling yourself whole and separate and yet with the world?

There is a tension in living fully, what often feels like an opposition between our longing for the solitude where we can find our own company and the desire to be fully and intimately with the world. When we learn to live with both the desire for separation and the longing for union, we find that they are simply two ways of knowing the same ache: we all just want to go home.

Some days, solitude is an impossibility. Caught up in the activities of daily living, I ache for my own company and am filled with a sorrow that makes me weep when I cannot find it.

And, at other times, I do too much and run too fast deliberately, unconsciously hoping to avoid the cool and steady gaze of that young woman standing on the patio, the gaze that sees clearly what is within and around me. Sometimes I don't like what she sees, don't like the company I keep when I am with myself, and want to pull away from this woman I am. So I fill the empty moments with TV, or work, or a book, or time with another. It takes courage to be willing to meet myself over and over again, seeing in my own face more beauty and grace and ability to love than I had hoped for, more judgment and impatience and need than I had feared. I forget that it does not matter how far or how fast I move, but only how much of myself I take along for the journey.

Fortunately, the illness that found me early in my adult life makes it impossible for me to move too far away from myself for too long. What was endured as curse is now my blessing. If I do not find a way to regularly create a place in my life for time that is empty, when nothing is scheduled or expected or reached for so I can be with myself, my glands swell, warning of an impeding descent into illness, calling me back to stillness.

And sometimes, when I find that sweet solitude, I hear warnings about isolation. Some summers, when I was alone in the wilderness, content in my tiny trailer at the edge of the lake, I would not speak to or see another human being for weeks. There, I could slow it all down. I felt the power of life being lived around and within me. I became like a sun-warmed rock in the center of the stream. The water parted around me, eddied in spirals, and flowed on, gently wearing away all my sharp edges.

Once, a man who was my lover and friend, and wanted to be more, came to see me there unexpectedly. I had just split an arm-load of wood and was carrying it into the trailer as he appeared. He stayed only briefly. Later he told me, "When I came down the drive-way and saw you standing there with the wood in your arms, your face glowing from the wind off the lake and the effort of chopping wood, I thought, 'She belongs to this place. She's at home here, alone in the bush. She's not missing me, doesn't need me here.' I felt like an intruder."

His observation surprised me. I heard the voice of my mother warning, "You are too independent. Don't get too good at being alone or you'll end up by yourself. Everyone needs someone."

Her fear finds a small corner in me, but I resist the idea that I will be with another only to avoid being alone. Surely, the ability to truly be with myself does not exclude the willingness to fully be with another. I do not seek isolation. The longing for another remains even when I am able to be with myself, although it is smaller, a whis-per that tugs at me gently. Even there, in my place of solitude in the wilderness, I found myself at moments wanting to turn to someone and share my awe at the brilliance of the full moon on the still water, the delight of watching the otters playing at the edge of the stream. But the loneliness was bittersweet and bearable because I knew myself and the world in a way I sometimes do not when I let my life become too full of doing things that do not really need to be done.

Once in a while, trying to find the end of the thread of what wants to be written, I will do a writing exercise that involves finishing the statement "I don't want to write about . . ." Over the years the statement is most often completed this way: "I don't want to write about the loneliness." For years I thought the loneliness, the longing for the other, was a weakness, a sign that I had not learned how to be with myself. And there have indeed been times when I have wanted to be with someone simply to cover the ache of not being able to find my own company. But I have come to accept that no matter how much I am able to be with myself, no matter how much I like my own company, I still long to sit close to and at times to merge completely with another in deep intimacy. This too is coming home. The completeness of self is found when we can be alone and when we can bring all of who we are to another, receiving and being received fully.

This is the sacred marriage: the coming together of two who have each met themselves on the road. When two who have this intimacy with themselves are fully with each other—whether for a lifetime or for a moment—the world is held tenderly and fed by the image they create simply by being together. They can be friends or family, lovers or life partners, or simply two strangers whose lives intersect for a moment. They may be telling each other stories, or making love, or sharing a task, or sitting in silence together. It doesn't matter. If, having met myself in the empty moments, I am willing and able to bring all of who I am to another, receiving all of who they are, then we are truly together. In that moment, in the image our being together creates, we are the manifestation of life holding, creating, and feeding life. This is the fullness of the homecoming for which we all long.

These moments, these sacred marriages of two, bring each person back to themselves more fully. When I was younger, the excitement of proximity and the heat of passion combined with an uneasiness with myself often meant that I lost myself when I was with another. When I was with someone who caught my imagination with possibilities beyond friendship, I found it hard to know what I wanted. I was aware only of his wanting me and was drawn by his desire.

Now that I am more able to be with myself, I seek those I can be with completely without losing myself. And when I listen for and follow the quiet but deep impulse to move toward someone— moving only as quickly as I can while staying connected to this impulse—I find a sweet ease in my body and an infinite tenderness in my heart. And I recognize what I have longed for in the nameless ache that has been with me for so many years. The tension eases between my desire for personal freedom and independence, my desire for the solitude of my own company and my longing for deep commitment and intimacy with others. I find, in our time together, more of myself. And I find, in my time alone, more of the world.

Tell me, how do you live with yourself and those around you? Are you willing to meet yourself and not turn away from what you see? Can you touch skin-to-skin when we meet, with just a word, a gesture, a moment of shared silence? Can you find your way home again and again, to the place where all the longing is met?

In the moments when we have come home to ourselves and the world, there is no fear, because we know what we belong to and what belongs to us.

When I was a teenager, I would walk home from choir practice in the evening, alone through the darkness, and I was not afraid. In the deep stillness of winter, with temperatures often colder than twenty below zero, I walked down silent streets between high banks of snow sparkling blue-white in the flickering glow of the northern lights. My breath hung in the air, small silver clouds of frozen moisture that came from my body. I was not afraid. I knew I belonged to the cold dark sky and the dancing lights. I knew I belonged to the people in the houses I passed—those I knew and those I did not. I knew I belonged to the snow-laden evergreens that bowed over the road. The only sounds were the crunch of my boots on the frozen ground and the soft, steady rhythm of my breath. And these belonged to me.

FLOWERING TREE MEDITATION

We are able to be alone with ourselves when we are aware of our individual vitality and our place in the world. This meditation has often helped me to find of place of deep contemplation, singular wholeness, and connection with the world around me.

Sit in a comfortable position with your back relaxed but straight. If you are in a chair, make sure that your feet are flat on the ground. Bring your attention to your breath, taking three large breaths in through your nose and exhale out through your mouth. Let your shoulders relax and drop down. On each exhalation, allow your weight to drop down into the bottom half of your body, letting go of any tension or tiredness.

Close your eyes. In your mind's eye, see the sun, gold and shining brilliantly, above you. Breathe the warmth and energy of the sun down through the top of your head, into your heart. Exhale this golden light down through your body and out through the base of your spine. Imagine a root coming out from the base of your spine, going down into the ground with each exhalation, fueled by the power of the sun. See it in your mind's eye going down into the moist brown earth beneath you, effortlessly moving down past boulders and underground streams, deeper and deeper into the coolness of the ground. Breathe the sunlight into your heart, and breathe out this root, seeing it extend a little more on each exhalation.

Now, imagine beginning to feel a tingling, a warmth at the end of this root as it nears the magma, the core of molten metal and rock at the center of the earth. Breathe this heat, the energy from the center of the earth, up along the root with each inhalation. Feel the root get warm and vibrate, bringing the energy up farther and farther toward your body with each inhalation. Feel this heat, this energy, enter your body, breathing it up through the center of your body, into your heart, and exhaling it from your heart, up through the top of your head. With each breath, breathe the power, the heat, and the light of the magma into your heart and exhale it through the top of your head, feeling yourself firmly rooted to the earth. Feel your body, like the trunk of a tree, bringing that energy up from the earth and sending it out through the top of your head as branches. With each exhalation see the branches in your mind's eye spreading out from the top of your head, lush and flourishing, reaching for the sky, filling with leaves. As you continue the cycle of energy, imagine the branches growing, arching above you and coming down on either side of you to touch the ground.

Sit and feel yourself at the center of this cycle of connection, breathing in the energy from the earth, up into your heart, and exhaling it out through the branches that return it to the earth where they touch the ground on either side of you. Be aware of your solid connection to the ground, of the strength of your body and the beauty and flexibility of the branches that grow out from the top of your head. From this place of wholeness and connection, open your mind and heart to thoughts of the world—its joys and its sorrows—neither reaching for nor hanging on to the thoughts that come, but simply observing them without judgment. Notice what thoughts and feelings about the world come to you—those about your own personal circles of family and friends and those about the world beyond your immediate circle. Feel yourself with the world even as you are here, alone and completely with yourself.

ACKNOWLEDGMENTS

Without community and Spirit in my life, this book would not have been written.

My heartfelt gratitude to my family—to my sons, Brendan and Nathan, for their constant encouragement, endless patience, and astute suggestions on the first draft; to my parents, Don and Carolyn House, for their help and love; to Linda Mulhall, sister of my heart, who is always there for me.

Thanks also to the circles of men and women to which I belong for their prayers and support—Kris Blok-Anderson, Suzy Gibson, Wendy Mortimer, Sara Weber, Philomene Hoffman, Mimi Yano, Ann MacPherson, Lise Tetrault, Judith Edwards, Lynley Hall, Judy Ann Smith, Liza Parkinson, Wende Bartley, Marie Claire Schacher, Ingrid Szymkowiak, Judith Cockman, Agnes Ohan, Lucinda Vardey, Suzanne Gregory, Hema Dias Abeygunawardena, Carol Sing Lun Mark, Ann Petrie, Pauline Faull, Maureen Campbell, Wilder Penfield, Brian Wheeldon, Peter Marmorek, Mitch Ross, John Jestadt, Carla Jenson, Myrna Mather, Margaret Carney, Vivien Cvetkovic, Catherine Jelinek, Cat Scoular, Ellen Martin, Elizabeth Verwey.

Thanks also to two shining stars of encouragement: Ellen Wingard and John O'Donohue.

I am very grateful to Peter and Judy Crawford Smith for their solid friendship and the hospitality of Bridgewater Retreat, a place of quiet beauty where I can write. Thanks to author David Whyte for the poetry and writing exercise that inspired both the meditation at the conclusion of the chapter entitled "The Longing," and the original "The Invitation." To Joe Durepos, my agent, I offer my gratitude for finding me and suggesting this book, offering me a much-needed structure for accumulated writing. My gratitude also to the folks at Harper San Francisco—in particular to my editor, Karen Levine, who made this process so painless that I was prompted at one point to seek reassurance that there were no unpleasant "surprises" I needed to anticipate. Thank you for ease.

"Thank you" feels inadequate to express my feelings to Catherine and Roger Mloszewski. You have allowed me to participate in, to be transformed by, and to share your story of tremendous courage and heart.

May the blessings of living fully flow to all these and to those I have not named who have touched me and taught me. My heart is full.

For information about Oriah's workshops and seminars, please write:

300 Coxwell Avenue
Box 22546
Toronto, Ontario
M4L 2A0
Canada

The Invitation

IT DOESN'T INTEREST ME WHAT YOU DO FOR A LIVING. I want to know what you ache for, and if you dare to dream of meeting your heart's longing.

It doesn't interest me how old you are. I want to know if you will risk looking like a fool for love, for your dream, for the adventure of being alive.

It doesn't interest me what planets are squaring your moon. I want to know if you have touched the center of your own sorrow, if you have been opened by life's betrayals or have become shriveled and closed from fear of further pain. I want to know if you can sit with pain, mine or your own, without moving to hide it or fade it or fix it.

I want to know if you can be with joy, mine or your own, if you can dance with wildness and let the ecstasy fill you to the tips of your fingers and toes without cautioning us to be careful, to be realistic, to remember the limitations of being human.

It doesn't interest me if the story you are telling me is true. I want to know if you can disappoint another to be true to yourself; if you can bear the accusation of betrayal and not betray your own soul; if you can be faithless and therefore trustworthy.

I want to know if you can see beauty, even when it's not pretty, every day, and if you can source your own life from its presence.

I want to know if you can live with failure, yours and mine, and still stand on the edge of the lake and shout to the silver of the full moon, "Yes!"

It doesn't interest me to know where you live or how much money you have. I want to know if you can get up, after the night of grief and despair, weary and bruised to the bone, and do what needs to be done to feed the children.

It doesn't interest me who you know or how you came to be here. I want to know if you will stand in the center of the fire with me and not shrink back.

It doesn't interest me where or what or with whom you have studied. I want to know what sustains you, from the inside, when all else falls away.

I want to know if you can be alone with yourself and if you truly like the company you keep in the empty moments.

From *The Invitation* by Oriah
Copyright © 1999 by Oriah Mountain Dreamer

Plus:

The Invitation

Plus: Insights, Interviews, and More

Writing "The Invitation"

Some days things unfold in my life in a way that makes me wonder why I am so certain that I need to diligently plan and work and try to make things come out right. Oh, I'm not suggesting that planning and working don't sometimes pay off, don't sometimes render hoped-for results. But when you find yourself following the impulse that comes from a deep stillness without the smallest thought or a shadow of an expectation about the outcome and then watch as things effortlessly unfold in a way you would not even have dared imagine, it makes you question all this trying, this dark certainty that everything must be earned or fought for. It makes you consider grace and the blessings of a human life that are ours simply by virtue of being alive. It opens you to the possibility of real surprises. It reminds you of how limited our perspective is, of how we often can't even imagine what is possible as we take a deep breath and plunge into another day, throwing a load of laundry into the dryer and stacking dirty dishes in the sink as we rush to make the morning bus, juggling deadlines at work against parent-teacher interviews, cringing as we vow once again that this will be the last time we pick up fast food or order pizza for dinner.

But sometimes, unexpectedly, a quiet moment finds us and we drop down into the life we have beneath all the rushing and the trying and the endless daily details, sinking into the fertile soil of the sometimes neglected inner life where the seeds of remembering what matters are planted. What comes from that place when we give it half a chance flows into our lives and the world creating unexpected changes in the direction of our journey and offering unanticipated blessings to us and those around us.

This is what writing "The Invitation" was like for me. It came in a quiet moment late at night when tiredness stopped my head from censoring the words that flowed from my heart onto the page. I had just returned from a party. I'm not good at parties. I always feel slightly confused standing around talking to strangers about things that don't really matter. I can't quite figure out what it is we're supposed to be doing. If we are celebrating something, someone's birthday or graduation or retirement, I want to do something together that will mark the occasion, have people offer prayers or stories or meditations that bring us into mindful awareness of the occasion and the person we are there to celebrate. And if we are there just to get to know one another, then I want to talk about things that matter, want to know how others feel about their daily lives, want to hear their hopes and disappointments, want to know what they think about just before they fall asleep at night, how they feel when their alarm clocks pull them up out of dreams in the morning. I'm not suggesting that my attitude toward parties is a necessarily a good one. There are times when I wish I understood the purpose and practice of just "hanging out" with others, but the whole thing

"What comes from that place when we give it half a chance flows into our lives and the world creating unexpected changes in the direction of our journey and offering unanticipated blessings to us and those around us."

Plus: **Insights, Interviews, and More**

eludes me. I'd rather take a walk in the woods or read a good book or have a hot bath. So most of the time I just don't go to parties.

But once in a while I worry a little about my inability to happily participate in what appear to be normal social activities. On this particular night, feeling this worry niggling at me, I'd convinced myself to go to the party, inwardly berating myself, "Oh for crying out loud, Oriah, just go to the party and try to be normal for a change. Not every moment has to be deeply meaningful and spiritually insightful! Just try chatting with people."

But it didn't work. Oh, it was a perfectly ordinary party and I'd done my best to behave myself, chatted with people without asking for or offering more than what was expected. But the familiar boredom mixed with confusion and frustration had once again set in as people stood around, drinks in hand, asking and answering the usual questions: What do you do? Where do you live? Who do you know? So I'd come home tired and disgruntled, more dissatisfied with social norms than with my own inability or unwillingness to conform to them.

Although this dissatisfaction with small talk is something that has always been with me, there was a reason why the feeling was so acute on this particular night in May of 1994. One year earlier on this day, standing in my kitchen cleaning and chatting with my dear friend Catherine, I'd watched as she'd suddenly raised her hand to her head complaining of a sharp pain. And as she'd winced I'd seen a flash of light, like the blinding

"And as she'd winced I'd seen a flash of light, like the blinding pop of a camera's flashbulb next to her temple. I can't explain it."

pop of a camera's flashbulb next to her temple. I can't explain it. Perhaps it was because my grandfather had had an aneurysm years before that the word immediately came into my mind like a silent and certain shadow filling me with dread.

There are events by which we mark our lives, usually unexpected and often tragic occurrences beyond our control that become a kind of watershed, all other events becoming known as that which came before or after. In North America Kennedy's assassination and September 11 are two such moments in our collective history. That day with Catherine became one of those reference points in my life. As I drove her to the hospital and she stopped breathing, as I reached out for her crying her name, as I sat in the hospital waiting room listening to the surgeon telling me he did not think he could save her, I felt everything I thought I knew turn to ash. A brain aneurysm is usually fatal and almost always unanticipated. One minute everything is as it has been, and in the next, everything is changed forever. Being with Catherine that day abruptly ended any temptation or tendency I had ever had to buy into comforting platitudes that promise unlimited control over our lives or pretend that we can know with certainty that everything happens, is caused or orchestrated by a higher power, for a worthy reason. It ripped from my hands and my heart my unacknowledged and only semiconscious belief in the power of my own will to protect myself and those I loved from any real harm with hard work and diligent practice. It brought the reality of impermanence, the reality of our own mortality and the consistency and unpredictability of change in our lives up against my face—hard. Catherine lived. Today she resides in a group home where she can receive the care she needs, continually working to improve her physical mobility and mental acuity. Despite her disabilities and all she has lost she continually expresses her gratitude for being alive.

One of the many things I received from that day with Catherine was a heightened sense of how none of us knows how much time we have. Any one of us could be, in this moment, sixty seconds or an hour away from a brain aneurysm. With this realization came a deepening of my desire to be fully present for every moment of this precious life I have been given. On the first anniversary of that day with Catherine, on the night I wrote "The Invitation," I was filled with wanting to make sure I did not waste one moment on that which does not matter, on small talk that does not really share anything or create any intimacy between us. Being with Catherine on that day a year before had split me open to my own longing to live from a deeper place, had given me the courage to allow the voice of what I ache for have its say.

So I sat down to write at my desk in the dim light of the street lamp outside my window. On this night I used a writing exercise I had received from poet David Whyte at a workshop over a year before. David had given workshop participants a writing exercise based on his poem "Self Portrait"

"Any one of us could be, in this moment, sixty seconds or an hour away from a brain aneurysm."

from his poetry collection *Fire in the Earth,* asking us to begin with the phrase, "It doesn't interest me...." and continue with "What I really want...." I had used this writing exercise dozens of times to go deeper in both my writing and my meditations, to discover what I did not already know about my own thoughts and feelings, to open to the ache I felt in my chest for something more.

As the words flowed I recognized a voice that has always been there within me: the voice that passionately seeks life's purpose; the voice of the tired heart that longs for real intimacy and deep rest; the voice that asks me to be fully present with it all—the pain and the joy, the beauty and the sorrow, the inner silence and the noise of the world. I wasn't the only one who recognized this voice as part of who I had always been. Later, after the prose poem had been unfolded into the book *The Invitation,* I received a letter from Jeff, a man I'd met when we were both teenagers on a canoe trip in Algonquin Park in Northern Ontario. Paddling together through the wilderness in the same canoe for two weeks, we had become each other's first love but had lost touch in the intervening thirty years. Finding my name and the prose poem on the Internet, he wrote to me, telling me he recognized "... the same tone of voice, the same clear thought that made my heart soar before I even knew what to do about it ..." all those years ago. It has been three years since I received this letter from Jeff. We were married eight months ago, and Jeff says he is grateful to love

> *"It has been three years since I received this letter from Jeff."*

Plus: **Insights, Interviews, and More**

and live with the only woman he knows who came with her own manual.

When I meet people at bookstore events they often ask me about my background. They want to know where the voice of "The Invitation" came from, what gave me enough faith in the longing to let it speak unfettered. I think we all have this voice and are given an underlying faith in its wisdom as our birthright. It is what gently prods us to remember that life is about more than just continuing. It is what calls us to be all of what and who we are in terms defined by our own soul's knowing instead of exclusively molding ourselves according to the culturally sanctioned drive for material success or any particular tradition's or teacher's definition of spiritual enlightenment. We each have this voice, although how it speaks to us, the words it uses, will differ and be shaped by the particular circumstances of our lives. The truth is that I am an ordinary woman with an extraordinary hunger, an ache to discover and consciously live the meaning of my life, and a conviction that that hunger can be satisfied only by cultivating a deeply spiritual life.

In the end, that is what "The Invitation" is about: a call from one heart to others to engage in life more fully together. "The Invitation" is the voice of my soul calling to you, to myself, gently reminding us that we ache for something more than just continuing, asking us to remember our capacity for deep intimacy, our ability to live the meaning at the center of our lives, to be aware of the Mystery that can hold it all.

"The Invitation" in the World

O n the day after the party, the morning after I had written "The Invitation," I was composing a newsletter to send out to students who had attended the retreats and classes I had offered over the years, and I decided to include the prose poem. I did not edit or rewrite it. I have in more recent years joked that had I known that so many people were going to read it I probably would have worked on it for days and ruined it or at least dulled the edge that sought to cut through to some truth beneath our usually polite and careful interactions. I often sent bits of my writing out to students. I wrote almost every day, and although I had had a book published by a small Canadian press four years earlier, the idea of wider publication, of making my living doing what I loved most—writing—seemed unlikely.

I sent off the newsletter that included "The Invitation" to the six hundred people on my mailing list. I heard back from a few who expressed their appreciation for the piece. At the time I was working on an old computer, a Mac SE. The slowness of the computer combined with my limited computer skills meant that while I had access to e-mail, I did not surf the Internet. So, it was several years before I found out what had been happening with "The Invitation," before I discovered the journey it had taken quite separately and independently

Plus, **Insights, Interviews, and More**

from me. In hindsight, what must have happened was that people on my mailing list had sent the prose poem to friends and acquaintances through e-mail, and it had spread. By the time I got online four years later there were literally thousands of Web sites displaying "The Invitation," some in strange and novel ways with unauthorized edits and unusual credits.

Slowly, as people began to track down who I was and where I lived, stories of how the poem had traveled began to trickle back to me. A woman in Africa wrote and told me that she had heard the poem read at a United Nations gathering there. Several people who had heard it at a spiritual gathering of about eight hundred people in New Zealand wrote asking for copies. I received e-mails from people in Iceland and Romania, South Africa and England, and from all over the United States and Canada. The Internet had indeed given the global villagers the ability to reach out and speak to one another.

In the midst of the stories about how the prose poem had come into people's lives I also heard about the assumptions and speculations that were being made about who I was. One man who had attended a men's retreat with Robert Bly wrote to me of his experience of hearing "The Invitation" read by one of the retreat participants. The several hundred men in attendance had responded in unison to each stanza with an enthusiastic "Ho!" the heartsound used in traditional Native American ceremonies to indicate "that speaks for me also!" Similarly I heard from a man who attended

"A woman in Africa wrote and told me that she had heard the poem read at a United Nations gathering there."

a weekly men's group in California where they began each meeting by reading "The Invitation." Although they had assumed I was a man, they continued to use the poem even after they found out I was a woman, and I was touched to be included in this way in their circle.

Initially my sons and I sent e-mails to people who had posted the prose poem on their Web sites with pictures of native elders in full headress and the description "Indian elder" after my name, attempting to clear up the confusion. It quickly became apparent that we could not keep up with the number of sites that were posting the poem. My sons took great glee in exploring new Internet territory daily and calling me to come and see new and sometimes truly bizarre sites where the prose poem was displayed. I finally decided to simply be grateful that so many were finding something in my writing that spoke to them and let go of even attempting to control how the piece was presented.

Although it made some sense to me that people thought I was Native American I was less able to understand those who took it upon themselves to change words in the prose poem, editing it to suit their own ideas. I suppose it is my own reverence for the written word that made this cavalier editing of someone else's work incomprehensible to me. But over time, although I made corrections where possible, I came to understand these anonymous edits as part of the conversation the poem was having with the world.

Stories continued to come in about where the prose poem was being used. People found beautifully

"It quickly became apparent that we could not keep up with the number of sites that were posting the poem."

Plus: **Insights, Interviews, and More**

printed copies propped in front of place settings at wedding receptions, heard it read by the valedictorian at their high school graduation, listened in tears as it was read at the graveside of a loved one. Therapists set copies out in their waiting rooms, recovery groups read it aloud together at the end of meetings, and speakers recited it in keynote addresses at conferences on everything from modern medicine to UFOs. In part I think because I live in Canada, I was completely unaware of most of this, did not know about the incredible journey this small piece of writing was taking until the whole things had been underway for several years.

Then one day I received a phone call from Joe Durepos, an American literary agent who was working at the time on behalf of Jean Huston. Jean wanted to include "The Invitation" in her upcoming book, *Passion for the Possible,* and I readily gave my consent. Joe asked me what else I had written. Since the publication of *Confessions of a Spiritual Thrillseeker* in 1990 I had done a lot of writing but had not been able to find a structure for another book. Joe asked me if I had thought of writing a book based on "The Invitation." The minute he said it I knew the prose poem offered the elusive structure I had been seeking. And so, following the ends of the threads in the writing I had accumulated, I began to unfold the prose poem, using separate chapters to go deeper into the longing expressed in each stanza. Joe became my agent and sold the manuscript to Harper San Francisco, and it subsequently became an international bestseller and was translated into over fifteen languages. Laith Al-Deen, a German pop star, wrote a song based on the translated lyrics for a CD produced by Sony World. All this from a few lines written late at night after a party!

With the publication of *The Invitation*, Harper San Francisco sent me on the road for a book tour, which enabled me to meet many of the readers who had in their enthusiastic sharing of the prose poem been responsible for its widespread distribution, an important factor in convincing a publisher to take a chance on an otherwise unknown author. The stories I heard about how the words I had written had come into people's lives and the impact they had had made me laugh and cry, made me wonder about the possibility of real magic afoot in the world.

There were countless stories of romance, of partners who connected through the poem. At one of the first bookstores I visited in California, a beautiful young woman eagerly approached me holding hands with a tall shy-looking man. "I want to tell you a story about your poem," she began, words I would hear from hundreds of people over the next few years. "My girlfriend sent it to me on the Internet and I loved it. I printed it out and took it over to my boyfriend's place, but when he read it he just shrugged and said, 'Yeah, OK. Doesn't do anything for me.' But when his roommate read it he thought it was great; he loved it as much as I did." She turned to the young man beside her." This is my ex-boyfriend's

Plus: **Insights, Interviews, and More**

roommate," she said, smiling the smile of a young woman in love, "and we're engaged to be married." We all laughed together.

There were, in addition to the lighthearted stories of romance, harder stories about how the prose poem had come into and impacted some lives. At one of my first bookstore appearances a young woman had approached me with a handmade plaque bearing the words of "The Invitation." She told me how her sister had committed suicide a year before, how she had not known how she would be able to continue in the midst of the grief and pain, had considered taking her own life. A friend had given her the poem and she had written it out and placed it beside her bed, reading it over and over when the darkness felt unbearable. "I do not think I would be here if it had not been for these words," she told me, choking back tears.

My initial inclination when I heard these stories was to push away the gratitude. I knew I could not take responsibility for what these people had received from the words I had written. I may on occasion have a moment of insight but I know that if I sat down to deliberately write something I thought would comfort someone who has suffered the loss of her child or the suicide of a dear sister or the deep despair that so often overtakes human beings, I would simply not know what to write. One day, listening to one of these stories of gratitude, and feeling myself pull away wanting to say, "It wasn't me," I finally got

"There were countless stories of romance, of partners who connected through the poem."

it. It's not about me! It's about what happens when we do our small part, when we bring ourselves to our lives as fully as we are able. When we are able to do this, if only for the hour it takes to put some words on a piece of paper, something happens that is larger than us, something that does not wholly come from us, something in which we are blessed to participate.

The most common comment I get from people writing to me about "The Invitation" is that it expresses something they have always felt and perhaps been unable to articulate. Over and over I hear, "How did you know? I feel as if someone has written about the things I think and feel that I do not tell anyone for fear of being rejected, of being found out as odd or different, as someone who wants too much."

This recognition of the self in another's story happens because we are more alike than different, all made of the same stuff, all wanting to love and be loved, to be seen for who we are, to find our happiness and live our lives fully. Strangely, unexpectedly, writing "The Invitation," allowing my own deep longing for real intimacy has opened me to an awareness of how there is no real separation between us, how we are all part of the same sacred life force finding its way, discovering itself in the shape of the human men and women we are.

And for this and all the other blessings "The Invitation" has brought into my life—I am grateful.

"I finally got it. It's not about me!"

Plus: **Insights, Interviews, and More**

OTHER BOOKS BY ORIAH

The Invitation

The book that started it all—Oriah exhorts us to fully examine our lives, learn to live with intimacy and joy, and, above all, be true to ourselves.

"*The Invitation* is a declaration of intent, a map into the longing of the soul, the desire to live passionately, face-to-face with ourselves and skin-to-skin with the world around us, to settle for nothing less than what is real."
—from the book

The Dance

The eagerly awaited follow-up to the surprise bestseller *The Invitation, The Dance* reveals how to let go and enjoy the dance of life. To dance, alone or with others, is to slow down and realize that who we are is enough.

The Call

In *The Call,* Oriah show us how to discover our unique role in the world. Each of us has our own call, our own specific place in the universe and a contribution that only we can make. But this call can be found only within ourselves.

Look for all three in a beautiful boxed set.